THIS F*CKING BUCKET LIST IS THE
CREATION OF

_____

AND   _____

_____

D1315248

IF FOUND, PLEASE CONTACT US URGENTLY:

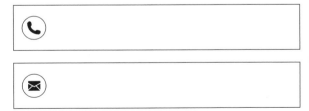

© 2020 Superior Notebooks

MASTER LIST

	BUCKET LIST ITEM	✓		BUCKET LIST ITEM	✓
1			26		
2			27		
3			28		
4			29		
5			30		
6			31		
7			32		
8			33		
9			34		
10			35		
11			36		
12			37		
13			38		
14			39		
15			40		
16			41		
17			42		
18			43		
19			44		
20			45		
21			46		
22			47		
23			48		
24			49		
25			50		

MASTER LIST

BUCKET LIST ITEM	✓	BUCKET LIST ITEM	✓
51		76	
52		77	
53		78	
54		79	
55		80	
56		81	
57		82	
58		83	
59		84	
60		85	
61		86	
62		87	
63		88	
64		89	
65		90	
66		91	
67		92	
68		93	
69		94	
70		95	
71		96	
72		97	
73		98	
74		99	
75		100	

EXPLORING GOAL SETTING

Name: _____   Name: _____

What personal characteristics or
traits are you most proud of?

What are some ways you could put
these personal characteristics into
action to achieve your goals?

Who inspires you? What of their
qualities and achievements do
you most admire? How could you
emulate these in planning your own
goals?

EXPLORING GOAL SETTING

Name: _____   Name: _____

Which works of art (books, music, art, poetry, movies or even TV shows) inspire you most? What parts of them do you admire most? How could they inspire your own personal goals?

It's never too late! What forgotten goals or dreams have you previously had that might be worth a revisit for 2020?

If a genie granted your dream goal today, what would your life look like? Describe in vivid detail!

EXPLORING GOAL SETTING

Name: _____   Name: _____

Define success for yourself when it comes to your goal. What tangible specifics (locations, dates, emotions, possessions, money, job status etc.) will exist when the goal has been achieved?

Focus on the journey! How will you feel after you've taken small steps towards your goal? How will you feel once you've achieved your quarter-way and half-way milestones?

Challenges and setbacks: How will you be gentle and forgiving if you should steer off-course? How would you redirect your focus to get back on track with your goals?

EXPLORING GOAL SETTING

Name: _____

Name: _____

What are some of your happiest memories? How could these moments inspire goals that inspire similar joy and gratitude?

What kinds of things may have prevented you achieving your goals previously? What will you do differently, or what resources will you need to ensure your new goals are achieved?

What impact will working toward, and achieving your goals have on loved ones? How will your success improve their lives?

GOAL SETTING WORD PROMPTS

1 ACCOLADE	57 CARING	113 DELIVER	169 FAR OUT	224 GRATITUDE	280 JOIN
2 ACCOMPLISH	58 CAROUSE	114 DELVE INTO	170 FASCINATING	225 GROUND	281 JOKE
3 ACCOMPLISHMENT	59 CAUSE	115 DESIGN	171 FASHION	226 GROUP	282 JOKING
4 ACCUMULATE	60 CELEBRATION	116 DESIROUS	172 FATHER	227 HALLOWEEN	283 JOYFUL
5 ACQUIRE	61 CEREMONY	117 DEVELOP	173 FEARLESS	228 HANG AROUND	284 JUBILATE
6 ACT	62 CHALLENGING	118 DEVISE	174 FEAST	229 HANG OUT	285 JUNKET
7 ACTION	63 CHANCE	119 DIFFERENT	175 FEAT	230 HAPPENING	286 KEEP
8 ACTUALIZE	64 CHARMING	120 DIG INTO	176 FEATHER IN CAP	231 HAPPINESS	287 KICK UP HEELS
9 AD-LIB	65 CHILDREN	121 DISCIPLINED	177 FESTIVITY	232 HARDY	288 LAND
10 ADVANCE	66 CHOOSE	122 DISCOVER	178 FETCHING	233 HATCH	289 LANDMARK
11 ADVENTURE	67 CHRISTMAS	123 DISHY	179 FIND	234 HAVE A BALL	290 LARK
12 AFFECT CHANGE	68 CIRCUMSTANCE	124 DISPORT	180 FINISH	235 HAVE A LOOK	291 LAUD
13 AGGREGATE	69 CLEANSE	125 DISPOSED	181 FIRE UP	236 HEAP	292 LAY FOUNDATION
14 ALLURING	70 CLUSTER	126 DISTINCTION	182 FIX	237 HEARTEN	293 LEAP
15 AMASS	71 COINCIDENCE	127 DISTRACTION	183 FLING	238 HEAVENLY	294 LET LOOSE
16 AMBITIOUS	72 COLLECT	128 DIVERSION	184 FLIRTATIOUS	239 HELP	295 LIBIDINOUS
17 AMBROSIAL	73 COLLEGE	129 DO	185 FLOCK	240 HEROIC	296 LINE
18 AMEND	74 COLORFUL	130 DONATION	186 FLYING	241 HOLIDAY	297 LIVE
19 AMUSEMENT	75 COME UP WITH	131 DREAM	187 FOLLOW	242 HOME	298 LIVE IT UP
20 ANNIVERSARY	76 COMPLETE	132 DREAM UP	THROUGH	243 HONESTY	299 LODGE
21 APPEALING	77 COMPOSE	133 DRINK TO	188 FOOD	244 HONOR	300 LONG SHOT
22 APPEARANCE	78 COMPUTER	134 DRIVE	189 FOOLERY	245 HOP	301 LOOK INTO
23 AROUSE	79 CONCEIVE	135 EAGER	190 FOREIGN	246 HOT	302 LOOK UP
24 ART AND DESIGN	80 CONCENTRATE	136 EARN WINGS	191 FOREST	247 HOTEL	303 LOTTERY
25 ASSOCIATE	81 CONCLUDE	137 EDUCATION	192 FORGE	248 HUDDLE	304 LOVE
26 ATHLETICS	82 CONCOCT	138 EFFECT	193 FORGIVENESS	249 HUMOR	305 LUSCIOUS
27 ATTAIN	83 CONFIDENT	139 ELATE	194 FORM	250 HUNT	306 LUXURY
28 ATTAINMENT	84 CONGREGATE	140 ELEVATE	195 FORMULATE	251 IMAGINE	307 MAGNIFICENT
29 AVANT GARDE	85 CONSECRATE	141 EMBOLDEN	196 FRAME	252 IMPRESS	308 MAKE
30 BABY	86 CONSTRUCT	142 EMPLOYMENT	197 FREEDOM	253 IMPROVE	309 MAKE MERRY
31 BEACH	87 CONTINGENCY	143 EMPOWERMENT	198 FRIENDS	254 IMPROVEMENT	310 MAKE OVER
32 BEAUTIFUL	88 CONVERGE	144 ENACT	199 FRISK	255 IMPROVISE	311 MAKE STRIDES
33 BETTER	89 CONVERSATIONAL	145 ENDOWMENT	200 FROLIC	256 INCIDENT	312 MAKE THE SCENE
34 BIKE	90 COOK UP	146 ENERGIZE	201 FULFILL	257 INCLINED	313 MAKE UP
35 BIKING	91 COOKING	147 ENHANCE	202 FUN	258 INCREASE	314 MANAGE
36 BIRTHDAY	92 COURAGEOUS	148 ENKINDLE	203 FUTURE	259 INDIVIDUAL	315 MARRIAGE
37 BIZARRE	93 COURSE	149 ENLIVEN	204 GAIN GROUND	260 INFLUENCE	316 MARVEL
38 BLESS	94 CREATE	150 ENTERPRISE	205 GALLANT	261 INFORM	317 MASS
39 BOLD	95 CREATIVITY	151 ENTICING	206 GALVANIZE	262 INFUSE	318 MATCH
40 BOOK	96 CROWD	152 ENVIABLE	207 GAME	263 INITIATE	319 MATTER
41 BOOST	97 CRUISING	153 ENVIRONMENT	208 GAMING	264 INQUIRING	320 MEET
42 BRAZEN	98 CUISINE	154 ENVISION	209 GARDEN	265 INSPECT	321 MEET AGAIN
43 BREAKTHROUGH	99 CULTIVATE	155 ESTABLISH	210 GENERATE	266 INSPIRIT	322 MEMORIALIZE
44 BRING ABOUT	100 CURIOUS	156 EVENING	211 GENEROUS	267 INSTALL	323 MEMORIES
45 BROTHER	101 CUTE	157 EVENT	212 GET DONE	268 INSTILL	324 MEND
46 BUCKET LIST	102 DALLIANCE	158 EXALT	213 GET TOGETHER	269 INSTITUTE	325 MERRIMENT
47 BUILD	103 DATING	159 EXAMINE	214 GIFT	270 INTERESTED	326 MILESTONE
48 BURROW	104 DAUGHTER	160 EXCITE	215 GIVE LIFE TO	271 INTOXICATING	327 MIRACLE
49 BUSINESS	105 DAUNTLESS	161 EXCLUSIVE	216 GIVE RISE TO	272 INTREPID	328 MOBILIZE
50 CABIN	106 DECISION	162 EXCURSION	217 GLAMOROUS	273 INTRODUCED	329 MONEY
51 CALL UP	107 DECORATION	163 EXHILARATE	218 GLOBAL	274 INVENT	330 MOOR
52 CAPER	108 DEDICATE	164 EXPEDITION	219 GLOBE-TROTTING	275 INVEST	331 MOTHER
53 CAPTIVATING	109 DEED	165 EXPERIENCE	220 GLORIFY	276 INVIGORATE	332 MOTIVATE
54 CAPTURE	110 DELECTABLE	166 EXTERNAL	221 GO INTO	277 INVITE	333 MOVE
55 CAR	111 DELICIOUS	167 EXTRAORDINARY	222 GOLD STAR	278 JEST	334 MOVEMENT
56 CAREER	112 DELIGHT	168 FALL/AUTUMN	223 GRANT	279 JOB TITLE	335 MOVIE

336 MUSIC
337 MUSTER
338 NAVIGATION
339 NEGOTIATE
340 NEPHEW
341 NERVY
342 NIECE
343 NOVEL
344 OBSERVE
345 OBTAIN
346 OCCASION
347 OCCUPATION
348 OCCURRENCE
349 OFF-THE-CUFF
350 ONE AND ONLY
351 OPPORTUNITY
352 ORDER
353 ORGANIZE
354 ORIGINATE
355 OUTLANDISH
356 OUTRAGEOUS
357 OUTSIDE CHANCE
358 OVERHAUL
359 OVERNIGHT
360 PAINT TOWN RED
361 PAINTING
362 PARENT
363 PARTY
364 PASS
365 PASSAGE
366 PASTIME
367 PATCH UP
368 PATIENCE
369 PAUSE
370 PEACEFUL
371 PECULIAR
372 PEREGRINE
373 PERFECT
374 PERFORM
375 PERFORMANCE
376 PERK UP
377 PERSEVERING
378 PERSISTENT
379 PHASE
380 PHENOMENON
381 PHOTOS
382 PICK UP
383 PILE UP
384 PLACE
385 PLAN
386 PLAY
387 PLEASING
388 PLEASURE
389 PLUCK
390 PLUCKY
391 POETRY

392 POKE
393 POLISH
394 POUR IN
395 PRACTICE
396 PRAISE
397 PRANK
398 PRECIOUS
399 PREPARATION
400 PREPARED
401 PROBE
402 PROCLAIM
403 PRODUCE
404 PROFIT
405 PROGRESS
406 PROJECT
407 PROMOTE
408 PROMOTION
409 PROMPT
410 PROPEL
411 PROSPECT
412 PROUD
413 PROVIDE
414 PROVOCATIVE
415 PUBLICIZE
416 PUNCH
417 PURIFY
418 PURSUIT
419 PUT
420 PUZZLED
421 QUESTIONING
422 QUICKEN
423 QUIET
424 RACK UP
425 RACY
426 RAFFLE
427 RAISE
428 RAISE HELL
429 RALLY
430 RAMBLE
431 RARE
432 REACH
433 REACTIVATE
434 READY
435 REALIZE
436 REASSEMBLE
437 REASSURE
438 RECESS
439 RECONCILE
440 RECONDITION
441 RECONVENE
442 RECOVER
443 RECREATE
444 RECREATION
445 RECTIFY
446 RECUPERATE
447 REFINE

448 REFORM
449 REFRESH
450 REFURBISH
451 REJOICE
452 REJOIN
453 REKINDLE
454 RELATIONSHIP
455 RELAXATION
456 RELIABLE
457 REMAKE
458 REMODEL
459 RENEW
460 RENOVATION
461 REPAIR
462 RESEARCH
463 RESOLUTE
464 RESOLVE
465 REST
466 RESTORE
467 RESURRECT

493 SCHOLARSHIP
494 SCOPE
495 SCORE
496 SCOUT
497 SCRIPT
498 SEAFARING
499 SEAL
500 SEARCH
501 SECURE
502 SEDUCTIVE
503 SEEK
504 SELF-CONFIDENCE
505 SELF-DRIVEN
506 SENSUAL
507 SET DOWN
508 SET IN MOTION
509 SET RIGHT
510 SET UP
511 SETTLE
512 SEXY

537 SPRING
538 SPRUCE
539 SPRUCE UP
540 SPUNKY
541 SPUR
542 STABILIZE
543 STACK UP
544 START
545 START BALL ROLLING
546 START OFF
547 STATION
548 STAY
549 STEAMY
550 STIMULATE
551 STIR
552 STOCKPILE
553 STOPOVER
554 STORY
555 STRAIGHTEN OUT
556 STRANGE

581 TRAVERSE
582 TREKKING
583 TRIP
584 TRIUMPH
585 TROPHY
586 TROPICAL
587 TRY
588 TURNING POINT
589 UNAFRAID
590 UNCOMMON
591 UNDERTAKING
592 UNFAMILIAR
593 UNFLINCHING
594 UNITE
595 UNIVERSITY
596 UNUSUAL
597 UP FOR
598 UPGRADE
599 UPLIFTING
600 VACATION

BUCKET LIST BRAINSTORMING: CLOSE YOUR EYES AND DROP YOUR PEN AT RANDOM (OR CHOOSE A NUMBER BETWEEN 1 AND 625). BRAINSTORM IDEAS BASED ON ONE OR MORE OF YOUR RANDOMLY CHOSEN WORD PROMPTS.

468 RETIREMENT
469 RETRIEVE
470 REUNITE
471 REVAMP
472 REVEL
473 REVERE
474 REVISE
475 REVITALIZE
476 REVIVE
477 RICHES
478 RIDE
479 RIDING
480 RING IN
481 RISK
482 RISQUÉ
483 ROMANCE
484 ROMANTIC
485 ROMP
486 ROUND UP
487 ROUSE
488 SABBATICAL
489 SAILING
490 SCARE
491 SCENE
492 SCHEME

513 SHAPE UP
514 SHARPEN
515 SHIFT
516 SHOT IN THE DARK
517 SIGHTSEEING
518 SIGN
519 SIRE
520 SISTER
521 SITUATION
522 SKILLS
523 SKYROCKET
524 SOJOURN
525 SOLVE
526 SON
527 SONG
528 SPARE MOMENTS
529 SPARE TIME
530 SPARK
531 SPAWN
532 SPEC
533 SPECULATION
534 SPICY
535 SPIRITED
536 SPORT

557 STRIKE
558 STRIKING
559 STUDY
560 SUAVE
561 SUGGESTIVE
562 SUMMER
563 SWARM
564 SWING
565 TAKE OFF
566 TALENTED
567 TEASING
568 TECHNOLOGY
569 TEST
570 THING
571 THRONG
572 THROW DICE
573 TIME MANAGEMENT
574 TIME OFF
575 TITILLATING
576 TOUCH
577 TOUCH UP
578 TOUR
579 TRANSIT
580 TRAVEL

601 VALIANT
602 VALOROUS
603 VENTURE
604 VIDEO
605 VISIT
606 VOYAGE
607 WAGER
608 WALK
609 WANDER
610 WANDERLUST
611 WARMTH
612 WAY OUT
613 WAYFARING
614 WEALTH
615 WEDDING
616 WEEKEND
617 WEIRD
618 WELCOMING
619 WIN
620 WING
621 WINTER
622 WONDER
623 WORK UP
624 WRITE
625 WRITING

MIND MAP

Start with a central idea or keyword (see "goal setting word prompts" on page viii) and work your way out, adding to the idea with variations (think: who? what? when? where?) or combine with other keywords to discover new possibilities.

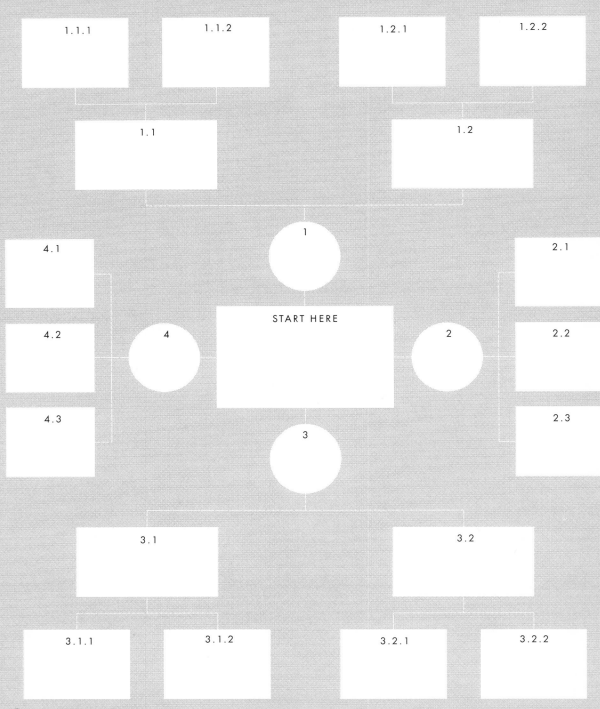

1.1.1

1.1.2

1.2.1

1.2.2

1.1

1.2

1

START HERE

4.1

2.1

4.2

4

2

2.2

4.3

2.3

3

3.1

3.2

3.1.1

3.1.2

3.2.1

3.2.2

TIP: Think about switching things up by combining your key idea with an unusual or unexpected time (classic example: Christmas in July). Time can include seasons, time of day, particular days of the week, months, anniversaries, birthdays and holidays.

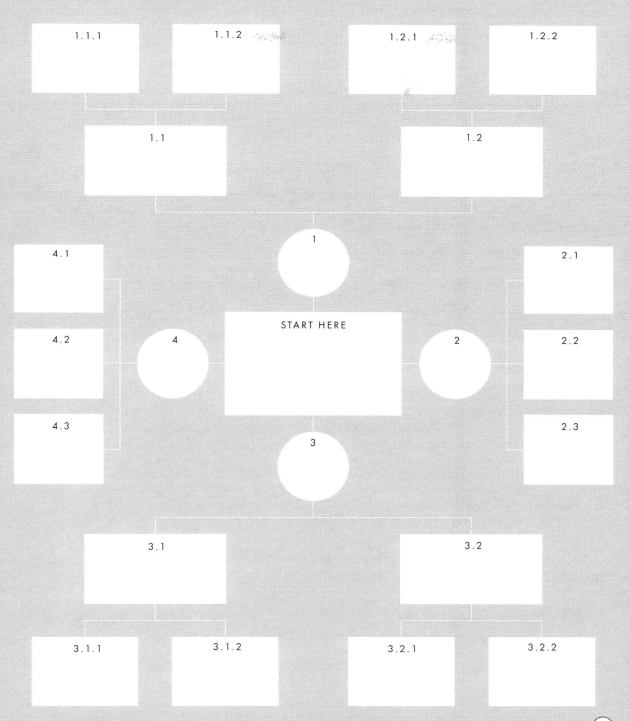

1.1.1

1.1.2

1.2.1

1.2.2

1.1

1.2

1

4.1

2.1

START HERE

4.2

4

2

2.2

4.3

2.3

3

3.1

3.2

3.1.1

3.1.2

3.2.1

3.2.2

MIND MAP

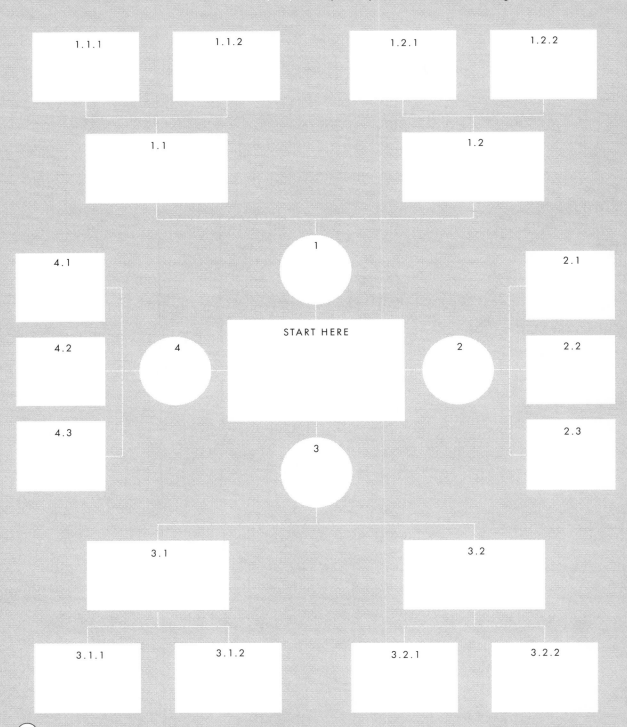

1.1.1

1.1.2

1.2.1

1.2.2

1.1

1.2

1

4.1

START HERE

2.1

4

2

4.2

2.2

4.3

2.3

3

3.1

3.2

3.1.1

3.1.2

3.2.1

3.2.2

MIND MAP

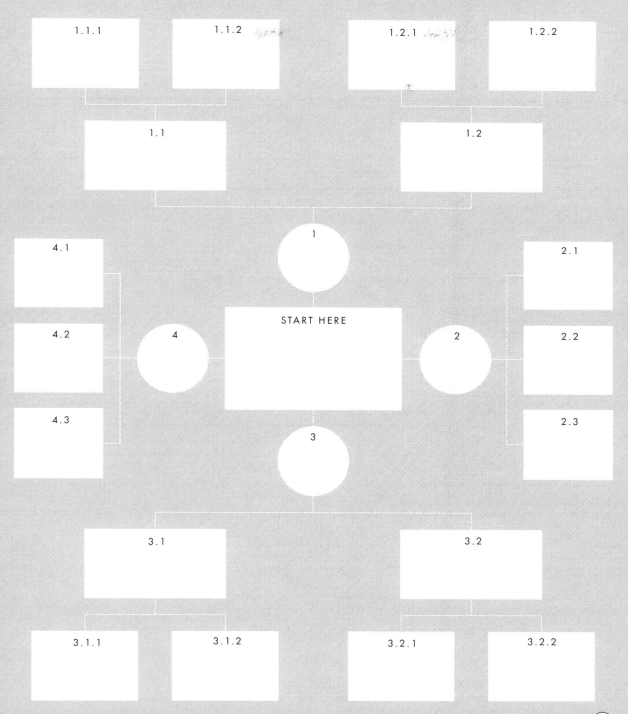

1.1.1

1.1.2

1.2.1

1.2.2

1.1

1.2

1

4.1

2.1

START HERE

4

4.2

2

2.2

4.3

2.3

3

3.1

3.2

3.1.1

3.1.2

3.2.1

3.2.2

MIND MAP

TIP: Don't get too caught up in technicalities or details when mind-mapping. Keep an open mind and allow spontaneity and intuition take over. Often it's the random or nonsense ideas that will lead you to something unexpected and amazing!

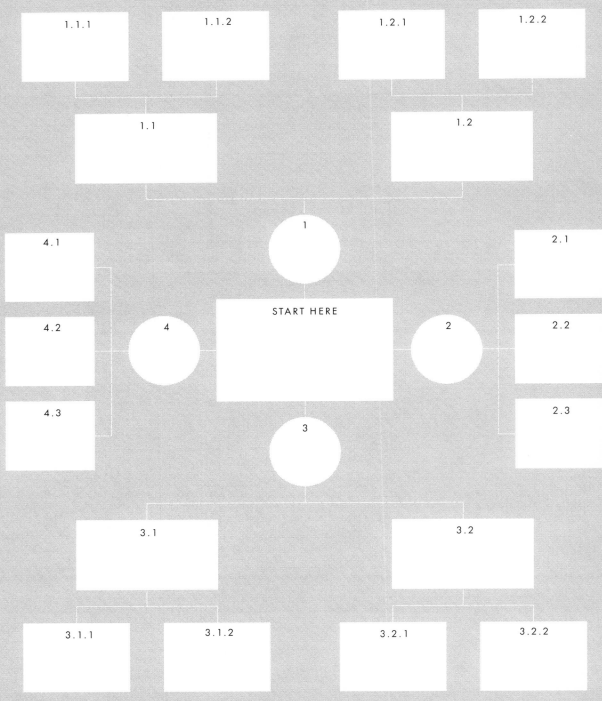

1.1.1

1.1.2

1.2.1

1.2.2

1.1

1.2

1

4.1

2.1

START HERE

4

4.2

2

2.2

4.3

2.3

3

3.1

3.2

3.1.1

3.1.2

3.2.1

3.2.2

MIND MAP

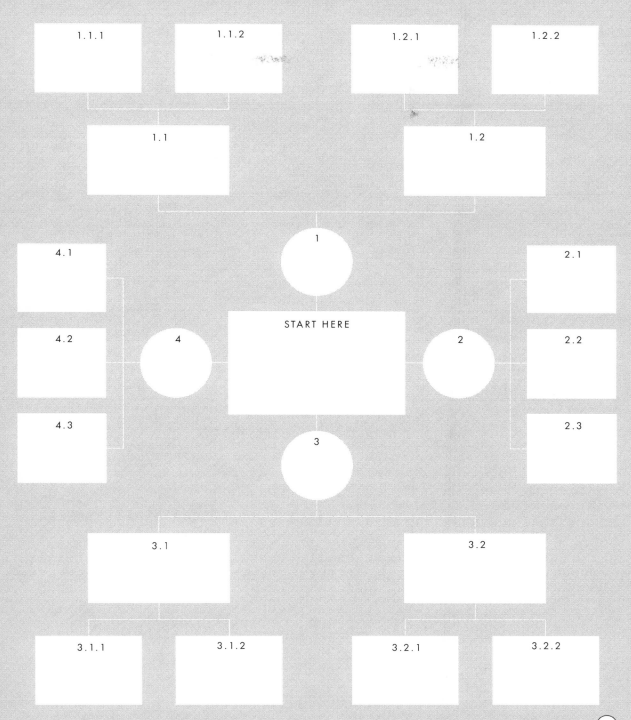

MIND MAP

TIP: Highlight the best ideas for further exploration. If you strike a golden bucket list idea, transfer it to a bucket list item planning page. From there work on fleshing out the challenge idea in terms of schedule, budget, and planning details to make it a reality.

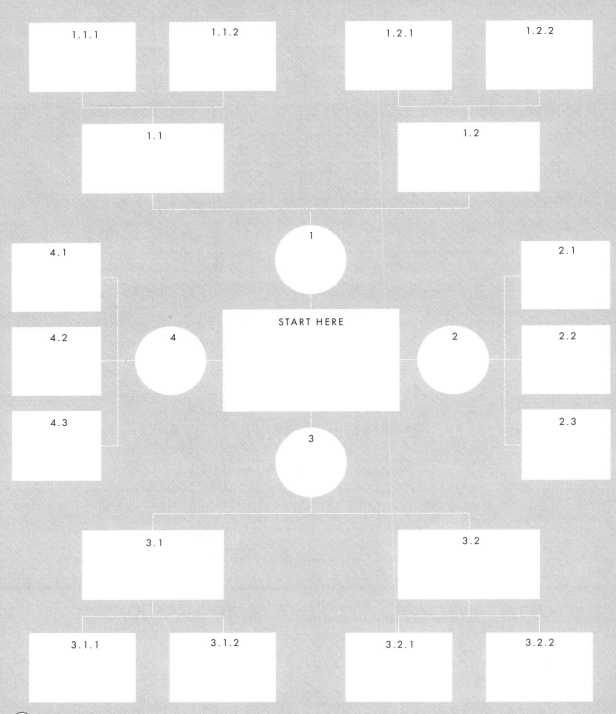

1.1.1

1.1.2

1.2.1

1.2.2

1.1

1.2

1

4.1

2.1

START HERE

4.2

4

2

2.2

4.3

2.3

3

3.1

3.2

3.1.1

3.1.2

3.2.1

3.2.2

TIP: How would money differentiate an idea? Think about switching around concepts of luxury and frugality to see how it would change an experience in an unusual way. 'Glamping' for example, combines the humble concept of camping with luxury.

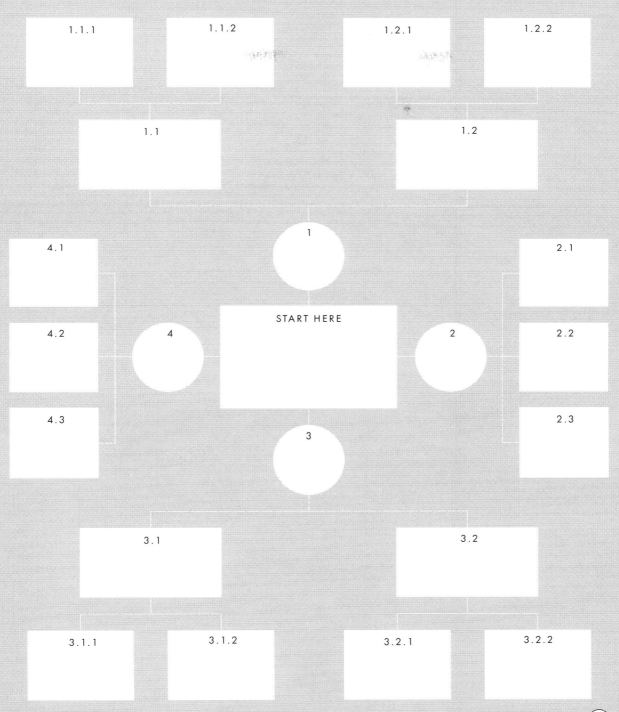

1.1.1

1.1.2

1.2.1

1.2.2

1.1

1.2

1

START HERE

4.1

4.2

4.3

4

2

2.1

2.2

2.3

3

3.1

3.2

3.1.1

3.1.2

3.2.1

3.2.2

MAJOR GOAL SUMMARY

This major goal is:

....

....

....

It will be accomplished by this date:

....

This goal is important to us because...

....

....

....

....

We will need to prepare the following resources to achieve this goal:

....

....

....

....

✒ **Goal Totem**

Insert a visual reminder (drawing, text, clipping)
that powerfully symbolizes this major goal.

MAJOR GOAL PROGRESS CHART

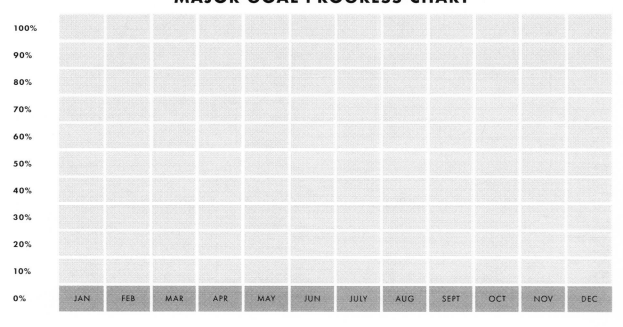

	JAN	FEB	MAR	APR	MAY	JUN	JULY	AUG	SEPT	OCT	NOV	DEC
100%												
90%												
80%												
70%												
60%												
50%												
40%												
30%												
20%												
10%												
0%												

MAJOR GOAL SUMMARY

This major goal is:

....

....

....

It will be accomplished by this date:

....

This goal is important to us because...

....

....

....

We will need to prepare the following resources to achieve this goal:

....

....

....

✎ **Goal Totem**

Insert a visual reminder (drawing, text, clipping)
that powerfully symbolizes this major goal.

MAJOR GOAL PROGRESS CHART

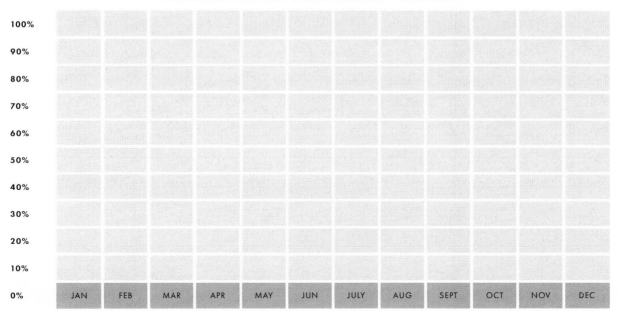

	JAN	FEB	MAR	APR	MAY	JUN	JULY	AUG	SEPT	OCT	NOV	DEC
100%												
90%												
80%												
70%												
60%												
50%												
40%												
30%												
20%												
10%												
0%												

MAJOR GOAL SUMMARY

This major goal is:

_____

_____

_____

It will be accomplished by this date:

_____

This goal is important to us because...

_____

_____

_____

_____

We will need to prepare the following resources to achieve this goal:

_____

_____

_____

_____

🖌 Goal Totem

Insert a visual reminder (drawing, text, clipping)
that powerfully symbolizes this major goal.

MAJOR GOAL PROGRESS CHART

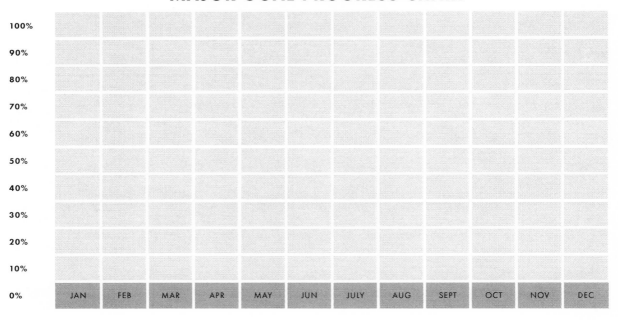

	JAN	FEB	MAR	APR	MAY	JUN	JULY	AUG	SEPT	OCT	NOV	DEC
100%												
90%												
80%												
70%												
60%												
50%												
40%												
30%												
20%												
10%												
0%												

MAJOR GOAL SUMMARY

This major goal is:

....
....
....

It will be accomplished by this date:

....

This goal is important to us because...

....
....
....
....

We will need to prepare the following resources to achieve this goal:

....
....
....
....

🖌 Goal Totem

Insert a visual reminder (drawing, text, clipping)
that powerfully symbolizes this major goal.

MAJOR GOAL PROGRESS CHART

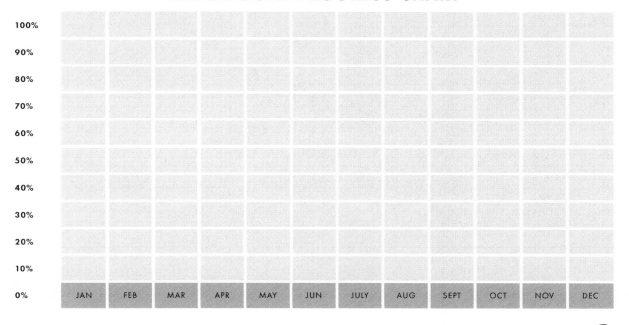

	JAN	FEB	MAR	APR	MAY	JUN	JULY	AUG	SEPT	OCT	NOV	DEC
100%												
90%												
80%												
70%												
60%												
50%												
40%												
30%												
20%												
10%												
0%												

MAJOR GOAL SUMMARY

This major goal is:

_____

_____

_____

It will be accomplished by this date:

_____

This goal is important to us because...

_____

_____

_____

_____

We will need to prepare the following resources to achieve this goal:

_____

_____

_____

_____

✎ Goal Totem

Insert a visual reminder (drawing, text, clipping)
that powerfully symbolizes this major goal.

MAJOR GOAL PROGRESS CHART

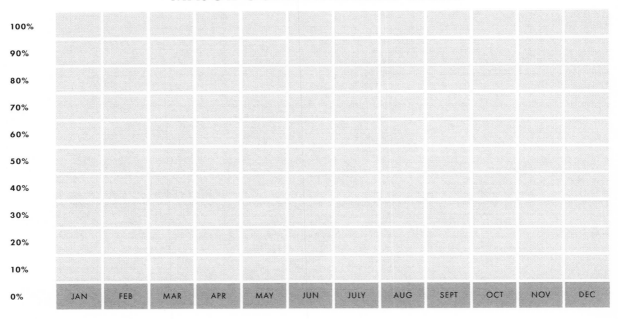

	JAN	FEB	MAR	APR	MAY	JUN	JULY	AUG	SEPT	OCT	NOV	DEC
100%												
90%												
80%												
70%												
60%												
50%												
40%												
30%												
20%												
10%												
0%												

The List

ITEM #1:

PRIORITY ★ ★ ★ ★ ★

SUMMARY: THIS WOULD BE F*CKING PERFECT FOR US BECAUSE...

_____
_____
_____
_____
_____
_____

BUDGET

$

ANTICIPATED DATE

/ /   TO   / /

ACTION LIST

- ⊘
- ⊘
- ⊘
- ⊘
- ⊘
- ⊘
- ⊘
- ⊘
- ⊘
- ⊘
- ⊘

MAKE IT F*CKING HAPPEN: HOW? WHEN?

_____
_____
_____
_____
_____
_____

REVIEW

DATE COMPLETED: / /

WHAT HAPPENED? (PEOPLE MET, HIGH POINTS, EXPECTATIONS VS REALITY)

_____
_____
_____
_____
_____
_____
_____
_____
_____

Success!

✓

ONCE COMPLETE, PLACE A CHECK HERE
TO TAKE IT OFF YOUR BUCKET LIST

RATE THIS ACTIVITY

★ ★ ★ ★ ★

ITEM #2:

PRIORITY ★ ★ ★ ★ ★

SUMMARY: THIS WOULD BE F*CKING PERFECT FOR US BECAUSE...

_____

_____

_____

_____

_____

_____

MAKE IT F*CKING HAPPEN: HOW? WHEN?

_____

_____

_____

_____

_____

_____

REVIEW

DATE COMPLETED: /   /

WHAT HAPPENED? (PEOPLE MET, HIGH POINTS, EXPECTATIONS VS REALITY)

_____

_____

_____

_____

_____

_____

_____

_____

_____

BUDGET

$

ANTICIPATED DATE

/   /   TO   /   /

ACTION LIST

○ _____
○ _____
○ _____
○ _____
○ _____
○ _____
○ _____
○ _____
○ _____
○ _____
○ _____

Success! ✓

ONCE COMPLETE, PLACE A CHECK HERE
TO TAKE IT OFF YOUR BUCKET LIST

RATE THIS ACTIVITY

★ ★ ★ ★ ★

ITEM #3:

PRIORITY ⭐⭐⭐⭐⭐

SUMMARY: THIS WOULD BE F*CKING PERFECT FOR US BECAUSE...

_____
_____
_____
_____
_____
_____
_____

MAKE IT F*CKING HAPPEN: HOW? WHEN?

_____
_____
_____
_____
_____
_____

BUDGET

$

ANTICIPATED DATE

/ /   TO   / /

ACTION LIST

- ⊘
- ⊘
- ⊘
- ⊘
- ⊘
- ⊘
- ⊘
- ⊘
- ⊘
- ⊘
- ⊘

REVIEW

DATE COMPLETED: / /

WHAT HAPPENED? (PEOPLE MET, HIGH POINTS, EXPECTATIONS VS REALITY)

_____
_____
_____
_____
_____
_____
_____
_____
_____

Success! ✓

ONCE COMPLETE, PLACE A CHECK HERE
TO TAKE IT OFF YOUR BUCKET LIST

RATE THIS ACTIVITY

⭐⭐⭐⭐⭐

ITEM #4:

SUMMARY: THIS WOULD BE F*CKING PERFECT FOR US BECAUSE...

_____

_____

_____

_____

_____

_____

_____

BUDGET

$

ANTICIPATED DATE

/ /   TO   / /

ACTION LIST

○ _____

○ _____

○ _____

○ _____

○ _____

○ _____

○ _____

○ _____

○ _____

○ _____

○ _____

MAKE IT F*CKING HAPPEN: HOW? WHEN?

_____

_____

_____

_____

_____

_____

_____

REVIEW

DATE COMPLETED: / /

WHAT HAPPENED? (PEOPLE MET, HIGH POINTS, EXPECTATIONS VS REALITY)

_____

_____

_____

_____

_____

_____

_____

_____

_____

_____

Success!

ONCE COMPLETE, PLACE A CHECK HERE
TO TAKE IT OFF YOUR BUCKET LIST

RATE THIS ACTIVITY

★ ★ ★ ★ ★

ITEM #5:

SUMMARY: THIS WOULD BE F*CKING PERFECT FOR US BECAUSE...

_____

_____

_____

_____

_____

_____

MAKE IT F*CKING HAPPEN: HOW? WHEN?

_____

_____

_____

_____

_____

_____

REVIEW

DATE COMPLETED: / /

WHAT HAPPENED? (PEOPLE MET, HIGH POINTS, EXPECTATIONS VS REALITY)

_____

_____

_____

_____

_____

_____

_____

_____

_____

_____

BUDGET

$

ANTICIPATED DATE

/ /   TO   / /

ACTION LIST

- ⊘
- ⊘
- ⊘
- ⊘
- ⊘
- ⊘
- ⊘
- ⊘
- ⊘
- ⊘
- ⊘

Success! ✓

ONCE COMPLETE, PLACE A CHECK HERE
TO TAKE IT OFF YOUR BUCKET LIST

RATE THIS ACTIVITY

★ ★ ★ ★ ★

ITEM #6:

SUMMARY: THIS WOULD BE F*CKING PERFECT FOR US BECAUSE...

_____
_____
_____
_____
_____
_____

MAKE IT F*CKING HAPPEN: HOW? WHEN?

_____
_____
_____
_____
_____
_____

REVIEW

DATE COMPLETED: / /

WHAT HAPPENED? (PEOPLE MET, HIGH POINTS, EXPECTATIONS VS REALITY)

_____
_____
_____
_____
_____
_____
_____
_____

BUDGET

$

ANTICIPATED DATE

/ /   TO   / /

ACTION LIST

- ⊘
- ⊘
- ⊘
- ⊘
- ⊘
- ⊘
- ⊘
- ⊘
- ⊘
- ⊘
- ⊘

Success!

ONCE COMPLETE, PLACE A CHECK HERE
TO TAKE IT OFF YOUR BUCKET LIST

RATE THIS ACTIVITY

★★★★★

ITEM #7:

PRIORITY ⭐ ⭐ ⭐ ⭐ ⭐

SUMMARY: THIS WOULD BE F*CKING PERFECT FOR US BECAUSE...

_____
_____
_____
_____
_____
_____
_____

MAKE IT F*CKING HAPPEN: HOW? WHEN?

_____
_____
_____
_____
_____
_____

BUDGET
$

ANTICIPATED DATE
/ /   TO   / /

ACTION LIST

- ⊘
- ⊘
- ⊘
- ⊘
- ⊘
- ⊘
- ⊘
- ⊘
- ⊘
- ⊘
- ⊘

REVIEW   DATE COMPLETED: / /

WHAT HAPPENED? (PEOPLE MET, HIGH POINTS, EXPECTATIONS VS REALITY)

_____
_____
_____
_____
_____
_____
_____
_____
_____

Success! ✓

ONCE COMPLETE, PLACE A CHECK HERE
TO TAKE IT OFF YOUR BUCKET LIST

RATE THIS ACTIVITY

⭐ ⭐ ⭐ ⭐ ⭐

ITEM #8:

PRIORITY ★ ★ ★ ★ ★

SUMMARY: THIS WOULD BE F*CKING PERFECT FOR US BECAUSE...

_____
_____
_____
_____
_____
_____

MAKE IT F*CKING HAPPEN: HOW? WHEN?

_____
_____
_____
_____
_____
_____
_____

REVIEW

DATE COMPLETED: / /

WHAT HAPPENED? (PEOPLE MET, HIGH POINTS, EXPECTATIONS VS REALITY)

_____
_____
_____
_____
_____
_____
_____
_____
_____

BUDGET

$

ANTICIPATED DATE

/ /   TO   / /

ACTION LIST

- ◯
- ◯
- ◯
- ◯
- ◯
- ◯
- ◯
- ◯
- ◯
- ◯
- ◯

Success! ✓

ONCE COMPLETE, PLACE A CHECK HERE
TO TAKE IT OFF YOUR BUCKET LIST

RATE THIS ACTIVITY

★ ★ ★ ★ ★

ITEM #9:

SUMMARY: THIS WOULD BE F*CKING PERFECT FOR US BECAUSE...

_____

_____

_____

_____

_____

_____

MAKE IT F*CKING HAPPEN: HOW? WHEN?

_____

_____

_____

_____

_____

_____

REVIEW

DATE COMPLETED: /   /

WHAT HAPPENED? (PEOPLE MET, HIGH POINTS, EXPECTATIONS VS REALITY)

_____

_____

_____

_____

_____

_____

_____

_____

_____

_____

BUDGET

$

ANTICIPATED DATE

/ /   TO   / /

ACTION LIST

- ⊘
- ⊘
- ⊘
- ⊘
- ⊘
- ⊘
- ⊘
- ⊘
- ⊘
- ⊘
- ⊘

Success! ✓

ONCE COMPLETE, PLACE A CHECK HERE
TO TAKE IT OFF YOUR BUCKET LIST

RATE THIS ACTIVITY

★★★★★

ITEM #10:

PRIORITY ★ ★ ★ ★ ★

SUMMARY: THIS WOULD BE F*CKING PERFECT FOR US BECAUSE...

_____

_____

_____

_____

_____

_____

BUDGET

$

ANTICIPATED DATE

/ /   TO   / /

ACTION LIST

MAKE IT F*CKING HAPPEN: HOW? WHEN?

_____

_____

_____

_____

_____

_____

_____

REVIEW

DATE COMPLETED: / /

WHAT HAPPENED? (PEOPLE MET, HIGH POINTS, EXPECTATIONS VS REALITY)

_____

_____

_____

_____

_____

_____

_____

_____

_____

Success!

ONCE COMPLETE, PLACE A CHECK HERE
TO TAKE IT OFF YOUR BUCKET LIST

RATE THIS ACTIVITY

★ ★ ★ ★ ★

ITEM #11:

SUMMARY: THIS WOULD BE F*CKING PERFECT FOR US BECAUSE...

_____
_____
_____
_____
_____
_____

MAKE IT F*CKING HAPPEN: HOW? WHEN?

_____
_____
_____
_____
_____
_____

BUDGET
$

ANTICIPATED DATE
/ / TO / /

ACTION LIST

- ⊘
- ⊘
- ⊘
- ⊘
- ⊘
- ⊘
- ⊘
- ⊘
- ⊘
- ⊘
- ⊘

REVIEW

DATE COMPLETED: / /

WHAT HAPPENED? (PEOPLE MET, HIGH POINTS, EXPECTATIONS VS REALITY)

_____
_____
_____
_____
_____
_____
_____
_____
_____

Success! ✓

ONCE COMPLETE, PLACE A CHECK HERE
TO TAKE IT OFF YOUR BUCKET LIST

RATE THIS ACTIVITY

★ ★ ★ ★ ★

ITEM #12:

SUMMARY: THIS WOULD BE F*CKING PERFECT FOR US BECAUSE...

_____
_____
_____
_____
_____
_____
_____

MAKE IT F*CKING HAPPEN: HOW? WHEN?

_____
_____
_____
_____
_____
_____
_____

REVIEW

DATE COMPLETED: / /

WHAT HAPPENED? (PEOPLE MET, HIGH POINTS, EXPECTATIONS VS REALITY)

_____
_____
_____
_____
_____
_____
_____
_____
_____
_____

BUDGET

$

ANTICIPATED DATE

/ /   TO   / /

ACTION LIST

- ⊘
- ⊘
- ⊘
- ⊘
- ⊘
- ⊘
- ⊘
- ⊘
- ⊘
- ⊘
- ⊘

Success! ✓

ONCE COMPLETE, PLACE A CHECK HERE
TO TAKE IT OFF YOUR BUCKET LIST

RATE THIS ACTIVITY

★ ★ ★ ★ ★

ITEM #13:

SUMMARY: THIS WOULD BE F*CKING PERFECT FOR US BECAUSE...

_____
_____
_____
_____
_____
_____

MAKE IT F*CKING HAPPEN: HOW? WHEN?

_____
_____
_____
_____
_____
_____

REVIEW

DATE COMPLETED: / /

WHAT HAPPENED? (PEOPLE MET, HIGH POINTS, EXPECTATIONS VS REALITY)

_____
_____
_____
_____
_____
_____
_____
_____

BUDGET
$

ANTICIPATED DATE
/ /   TO   / /

ACTION LIST

- ⊘
- ⊘
- ⊘
- ⊘
- ⊘
- ⊘
- ⊘
- ⊘
- ⊘
- ⊘
- ⊘

Success!

ONCE COMPLETE, PLACE A CHECK HERE
TO TAKE IT OFF YOUR BUCKET LIST

RATE THIS ACTIVITY

★★★★★

ITEM #14:

SUMMARY: THIS WOULD BE F*CKING PERFECT FOR US BECAUSE...

_____
_____
_____
_____
_____
_____
_____

BUDGET

$

ANTICIPATED DATE

/ /   TO   / /

ACTION LIST

○ _____
○ _____
○ _____
○ _____
○ _____
○ _____
○ _____
○ _____
○ _____
○ _____

MAKE IT F*CKING HAPPEN: HOW? WHEN?

_____
_____
_____
_____
_____
_____
_____

REVIEW

DATE COMPLETED: / /

WHAT HAPPENED? (PEOPLE MET, HIGH POINTS, EXPECTATIONS VS REALITY)

_____
_____
_____
_____
_____
_____
_____
_____
_____

Success! ✓

ONCE COMPLETE, PLACE A CHECK HERE
TO TAKE IT OFF YOUR BUCKET LIST

RATE THIS ACTIVITY

★ ★ ★ ★ ★

ITEM #15:

SUMMARY: THIS WOULD BE F*CKING PERFECT FOR US BECAUSE...

_____

_____

_____

_____

_____

_____

_____

MAKE IT F*CKING HAPPEN: HOW? WHEN?

_____

_____

_____

_____

_____

_____

_____

BUDGET
$

ANTICIPATED DATE
/ / TO / /

ACTION LIST

- ⊘ _____
- ⊘ _____
- ⊘ _____
- ⊘ _____
- ⊘ _____
- ⊘ _____
- ⊘ _____
- ⊘ _____
- ⊘ _____
- ⊘ _____
- ⊘ _____

REVIEW

DATE COMPLETED: / /

WHAT HAPPENED? (PEOPLE MET, HIGH POINTS, EXPECTATIONS VS REALITY)

_____

_____

_____

_____

_____

_____

_____

_____

_____

_____

Success!

ONCE COMPLETE, PLACE A CHECK HERE
TO TAKE IT OFF YOUR BUCKET LIST

RATE THIS ACTIVITY

★ ★ ★ ★ ★

ITEM #16:

PRIORITY ★ ★ ★ ★ ★

SUMMARY: THIS WOULD BE F*CKING PERFECT FOR US BECAUSE...

_____

_____

_____

_____

_____

_____

MAKE IT F*CKING HAPPEN: HOW? WHEN?

_____

_____

_____

_____

_____

_____

REVIEW

DATE COMPLETED: / /

WHAT HAPPENED? (PEOPLE MET, HIGH POINTS, EXPECTATIONS VS REALITY)

_____

_____

_____

_____

_____

_____

_____

_____

BUDGET

$

ANTICIPATED DATE

/ /   TO   / /

ACTION LIST

- ⊘
- ⊘
- ⊘
- ⊘
- ⊘
- ⊘
- ⊘
- ⊘
- ⊘
- ⊘
- ⊘

Success! ✓

ONCE COMPLETE, PLACE A CHECK HERE
TO TAKE IT OFF YOUR BUCKET LIST

RATE THIS ACTIVITY

★ ★ ★ ★ ★

ITEM #17:

SUMMARY: THIS WOULD BE F*CKING PERFECT FOR US BECAUSE...

_____

_____

_____

_____

_____

_____

MAKE IT F*CKING HAPPEN: HOW? WHEN?

_____

_____

_____

_____

_____

_____

REVIEW

DATE COMPLETED: / /

WHAT HAPPENED? (PEOPLE MET, HIGH POINTS, EXPECTATIONS VS REALITY)

_____

_____

_____

_____

_____

_____

_____

_____

BUDGET

$

ANTICIPATED DATE

/ /   TO   / /

ACTION LIST

- ⊘
- ⊘
- ⊘
- ⊘
- ⊘
- ⊘
- ⊘
- ⊘
- ⊘
- ⊘
- ⊘

Success! ✓

ONCE COMPLETE, PLACE A CHECK HERE
TO TAKE IT OFF YOUR BUCKET LIST

RATE THIS ACTIVITY

★★★★★

ITEM #18:

SUMMARY: THIS WOULD BE F*CKING PERFECT FOR US BECAUSE...

_____

_____

_____

_____

_____

_____

MAKE IT F*CKING HAPPEN: HOW? WHEN?

_____

_____

_____

_____

_____

_____

BUDGET

$

ANTICIPATED DATE

/ /   TO   / /

ACTION LIST

- ⊘
- ⊘
- ⊘
- ⊘
- ⊘
- ⊘
- ⊘
- ⊘
- ⊘
- ⊘
- ⊘

REVIEW

DATE COMPLETED: / /

WHAT HAPPENED? (PEOPLE MET, HIGH POINTS, EXPECTATIONS VS REALITY)

_____

_____

_____

_____

_____

_____

_____

_____

_____

_____

Success!

ONCE COMPLETE, PLACE A CHECK HERE
TO TAKE IT OFF YOUR BUCKET LIST

RATE THIS ACTIVITY

★ ★ ★ ★ ★

ITEM #19:

PRIORITY ★ ★ ★ ★ ★

SUMMARY: THIS WOULD BE F*CKING PERFECT FOR US BECAUSE...

_____
_____
_____
_____
_____
_____
_____

MAKE IT F*CKING HAPPEN: HOW? WHEN?

_____
_____
_____
_____
_____
_____

REVIEW

DATE COMPLETED: /   /

WHAT HAPPENED? (PEOPLE MET, HIGH POINTS, EXPECTATIONS VS REALITY)

_____
_____
_____
_____
_____
_____
_____
_____
_____

BUDGET

$

ANTICIPATED DATE

/   /   TO   /   /

ACTION LIST

- ⊘
- ⊘
- ⊘
- ⊘
- ⊘
- ⊘
- ⊘
- ⊘
- ⊘
- ⊘
- ⊘

Success!

✓

ONCE COMPLETE, PLACE A CHECK HERE
TO TAKE IT OFF YOUR BUCKET LIST

RATE THIS ACTIVITY

★ ★ ★ ★ ★

ITEM #20:

SUMMARY: THIS WOULD BE F*CKING PERFECT FOR US BECAUSE...

_____

_____

_____

_____

_____

_____

MAKE IT F*CKING HAPPEN: HOW? WHEN?

_____

_____

_____

_____

_____

_____

_____

REVIEW

DATE COMPLETED: / /

WHAT HAPPENED? (PEOPLE MET, HIGH POINTS, EXPECTATIONS VS REALITY)

_____

_____

_____

_____

_____

_____

_____

_____

_____

BUDGET

$

ANTICIPATED DATE

/ /   TO   / /

ACTION LIST

- ⊘
- ⊘
- ⊘
- ⊘
- ⊘
- ⊘
- ⊘
- ⊘
- ⊘
- ⊘
- ⊘

Success! ✓

ONCE COMPLETE, PLACE A CHECK HERE
TO TAKE IT OFF YOUR BUCKET LIST

RATE THIS ACTIVITY

★ ★ ★ ★ ★

ITEM #21:

SUMMARY: THIS WOULD BE F*CKING PERFECT FOR US BECAUSE...

_____

_____

_____

_____

_____

_____

_____

MAKE IT F*CKING HAPPEN: HOW? WHEN?

_____

_____

_____

_____

_____

_____

REVIEW

DATE COMPLETED: / /

WHAT HAPPENED? (PEOPLE MET, HIGH POINTS, EXPECTATIONS VS REALITY)

_____

_____

_____

_____

_____

_____

_____

_____

_____

_____

BUDGET

$

ANTICIPATED DATE

/ /   TO   / /

ACTION LIST

- ⊘
- ⊘
- ⊘
- ⊘
- ⊘
- ⊘
- ⊘
- ⊘
- ⊘
- ⊘
- ⊘

Success!

ONCE COMPLETE, PLACE A CHECK HERE
TO TAKE IT OFF YOUR BUCKET LIST

RATE THIS ACTIVITY

★★★★★

ITEM #22:

PRIORITY ★ ★ ★ ★ ★

SUMMARY: THIS WOULD BE F*CKING PERFECT FOR US BECAUSE...

_____
_____
_____
_____
_____
_____
_____

MAKE IT F*CKING HAPPEN: HOW? WHEN?

_____
_____
_____
_____
_____
_____

BUDGET

$

ANTICIPATED DATE

/ /   TO   / /

ACTION LIST

⊘ _____
⊘ _____
⊘ _____
⊘ _____
⊘ _____
⊘ _____
⊘ _____
⊘ _____
⊘ _____
⊘ _____
⊘

REVIEW

DATE COMPLETED: / /

WHAT HAPPENED? (PEOPLE MET, HIGH POINTS, EXPECTATIONS VS REALITY)

_____
_____
_____
_____
_____
_____
_____
_____
_____

Success!

✓

ONCE COMPLETE, PLACE A CHECK HERE
TO TAKE IT OFF YOUR BUCKET LIST

RATE THIS ACTIVITY

★ ★ ★ ★ ★

ITEM #23:

PRIORITY ★ ★ ★ ★ ★

SUMMARY: THIS WOULD BE F*CKING PERFECT FOR US BECAUSE...

_____
_____
_____
_____
_____
_____
_____

BUDGET

$

ANTICIPATED DATE

/ / TO / /

ACTION LIST

MAKE IT F*CKING HAPPEN: HOW? WHEN?

_____
_____
_____
_____
_____
_____
_____

REVIEW

DATE COMPLETED: / /

WHAT HAPPENED? (PEOPLE MET, HIGH POINTS, EXPECTATIONS VS REALITY)

_____
_____
_____
_____
_____
_____
_____
_____
_____

Success!

ONCE COMPLETE, PLACE A CHECK HERE
TO TAKE IT OFF YOUR BUCKET LIST

RATE THIS ACTIVITY

★ ★ ★ ★ ★

ITEM #24:

PRIORITY ★ ★ ★ ★ ★

SUMMARY: THIS WOULD BE F*CKING PERFECT FOR US BECAUSE...

_____

_____

_____

_____

_____

_____

_____

MAKE IT F*CKING HAPPEN: HOW? WHEN?

_____

_____

_____

_____

_____

_____

_____

BUDGET

$

ANTICIPATED DATE

/ /   TO   / /

ACTION LIST

⊘ _____

⊘ _____

⊘ _____

⊘ _____

⊘ _____

⊘ _____

⊘ _____

⊘ _____

⊘ _____

⊘ _____

⊘ _____

REVIEW

DATE COMPLETED: / /

WHAT HAPPENED? (PEOPLE MET, HIGH POINTS, EXPECTATIONS VS REALITY)

_____

_____

_____

_____

_____

_____

_____

_____

_____

_____

_____

Success!

✓

ONCE COMPLETE, PLACE A CHECK HERE
TO TAKE IT OFF YOUR BUCKET LIST

RATE THIS ACTIVITY

★ ★ ★ ★ ★

ITEM #25:

PRIORITY ★ ★ ★ ★ ★

SUMMARY: THIS WOULD BE F*CKING PERFECT FOR US BECAUSE...

_____
_____
_____
_____
_____
_____

MAKE IT F*CKING HAPPEN: HOW? WHEN?

_____
_____
_____
_____
_____
_____

BUDGET
$

ANTICIPATED DATE
/ /   TO   / /

ACTION LIST

- ⊘
- ⊘
- ⊘
- ⊘
- ⊘
- ⊘
- ⊘
- ⊘
- ⊘
- ⊘
- ⊘

REVIEW

DATE COMPLETED: / /

WHAT HAPPENED? (PEOPLE MET, HIGH POINTS, EXPECTATIONS VS REALITY)

_____
_____
_____
_____
_____
_____
_____
_____
_____

Success!

ONCE COMPLETE, PLACE A CHECK HERE
TO TAKE IT OFF YOUR BUCKET LIST

RATE THIS ACTIVITY

★ ★ ★ ★ ★

ITEM #26:

SUMMARY: THIS WOULD BE F*CKING PERFECT FOR US BECAUSE...

_____
_____
_____
_____
_____
_____

MAKE IT F*CKING HAPPEN: HOW? WHEN?

_____
_____
_____
_____
_____
_____

BUDGET

$

ANTICIPATED DATE

/ /   TO   / /

ACTION LIST

- ◯
- ◯
- ◯
- ◯
- ◯
- ◯
- ◯
- ◯
- ◯
- ◯

REVIEW

DATE COMPLETED: / /

WHAT HAPPENED? (PEOPLE MET, HIGH POINTS, EXPECTATIONS VS REALITY)

_____
_____
_____
_____
_____
_____
_____
_____

Success! ✓

ONCE COMPLETE, PLACE A CHECK HERE
TO TAKE IT OFF YOUR BUCKET LIST

RATE THIS ACTIVITY

★ ★ ★ ★ ★

ITEM #27:

PRIORITY ★ ★ ★ ★ ★

SUMMARY: THIS WOULD BE F*CKING PERFECT FOR US BECAUSE...

_____
_____
_____
_____
_____
_____
_____

BUDGET
$

ANTICIPATED DATE
/ /   TO   / /

ACTION LIST

○ _____
○ _____
○ _____
○ _____
○ _____
○ _____
○ _____
○ _____
○ _____
○ _____
○ _____

MAKE IT F*CKING HAPPEN: HOW? WHEN?

_____
_____
_____
_____
_____
_____

REVIEW

DATE COMPLETED: / /

WHAT HAPPENED? (PEOPLE MET, HIGH POINTS, EXPECTATIONS VS REALITY)

_____
_____
_____
_____
_____
_____
_____
_____
_____
_____

Success!

✓

ONCE COMPLETE, PLACE A CHECK HERE
TO TAKE IT OFF YOUR BUCKET LIST

RATE THIS ACTIVITY

★ ★ ★ ★ ★

ITEM #28:

SUMMARY: THIS WOULD BE F*CKING PERFECT FOR US BECAUSE...

_____
_____
_____
_____
_____
_____

MAKE IT F*CKING HAPPEN: HOW? WHEN?

_____
_____
_____
_____
_____
_____

REVIEW

DATE COMPLETED: / /

WHAT HAPPENED? (PEOPLE MET, HIGH POINTS, EXPECTATIONS VS REALITY)

_____
_____
_____
_____
_____
_____
_____
_____
_____

BUDGET

$

ANTICIPATED DATE

/ /   TO   / /

ACTION LIST

- ⊘
- ⊘
- ⊘
- ⊘
- ⊘
- ⊘
- ⊘
- ⊘
- ⊘
- ⊘
- ⊘

Success!

ONCE COMPLETE, PLACE A CHECK HERE
TO TAKE IT OFF YOUR BUCKET LIST

RATE THIS ACTIVITY

★★★★★

28

ITEM #29:

PRIORITY ★★★★★

SUMMARY: THIS WOULD BE F*CKING PERFECT FOR US BECAUSE...

_____
_____
_____
_____
_____
_____
_____

MAKE IT F*CKING HAPPEN: HOW? WHEN?

_____
_____
_____
_____
_____
_____
_____
_____

BUDGET

$

ANTICIPATED DATE

/ /   TO   / /

ACTION LIST

- ⊘
- ⊘
- ⊘
- ⊘
- ⊘
- ⊘
- ⊘
- ⊘
- ⊘
- ⊘
- ⊘

REVIEW

DATE COMPLETED: / /

WHAT HAPPENED? (PEOPLE MET, HIGH POINTS, EXPECTATIONS VS REALITY)

_____
_____
_____
_____
_____
_____
_____
_____
_____
_____

Success! ✓

ONCE COMPLETE, PLACE A CHECK HERE
TO TAKE IT OFF YOUR BUCKET LIST

RATE THIS ACTIVITY

★★★★★

ITEM #30:

SUMMARY: THIS WOULD BE F*CKING PERFECT FOR US BECAUSE...

_____
_____
_____
_____
_____
_____
_____

MAKE IT F*CKING HAPPEN: HOW? WHEN?

_____
_____
_____
_____
_____
_____
_____

REVIEW

DATE COMPLETED: / /

WHAT HAPPENED? (PEOPLE MET, HIGH POINTS, EXPECTATIONS VS REALITY)

_____
_____
_____
_____
_____
_____
_____
_____
_____

BUDGET

$

ANTICIPATED DATE

/ /   TO   / /

ACTION LIST

○ _____
○ _____
○ _____
○ _____
○ _____
○ _____
○ _____
○ _____
○ _____
○ _____
○ _____

Success! ✓

ONCE COMPLETE, PLACE A CHECK HERE
TO TAKE IT OFF YOUR BUCKET LIST

RATE THIS ACTIVITY

★ ★ ★ ★ ★

ITEM #31:

SUMMARY: THIS WOULD BE F*CKING PERFECT FOR US BECAUSE...

_____

_____

_____

_____

_____

_____

MAKE IT F*CKING HAPPEN: HOW? WHEN?

_____

_____

_____

_____

_____

_____

BUDGET

$

ANTICIPATED DATE

/ /   TO   / /

ACTION LIST

- ⊘
- ⊘
- ⊘
- ⊘
- ⊘
- ⊘
- ⊘
- ⊘
- ⊘
- ⊘
- ⊘

REVIEW

DATE COMPLETED: / /

WHAT HAPPENED? (PEOPLE MET, HIGH POINTS, EXPECTATIONS VS REALITY)

_____

_____

_____

_____

_____

_____

_____

_____

Success! ✓

ONCE COMPLETE, PLACE A CHECK HERE
TO TAKE IT OFF YOUR BUCKET LIST

RATE THIS ACTIVITY

★ ★ ★ ★ ★

ITEM #32:

SUMMARY: THIS WOULD BE F*CKING PERFECT FOR US BECAUSE...

_____
_____
_____
_____
_____
_____
_____

BUDGET

$

ANTICIPATED DATE

/ /   TO   / /

ACTION LIST

○ _____
○ _____
○ _____
○ _____
○ _____
○ _____
○ _____
○ _____
○ _____
○ _____
○ _____

MAKE IT F*CKING HAPPEN: HOW? WHEN?

_____
_____
_____
_____
_____
_____
_____

REVIEW

DATE COMPLETED: / /

WHAT HAPPENED? (PEOPLE MET, HIGH POINTS, EXPECTATIONS VS REALITY)

_____
_____
_____
_____
_____
_____
_____
_____
_____
_____
_____

Success!

✓

ONCE COMPLETE, PLACE A CHECK HERE
TO TAKE IT OFF YOUR BUCKET LIST

RATE THIS ACTIVITY

★ ★ ★ ★ ★

ITEM #33:

SUMMARY: THIS WOULD BE F*CKING PERFECT FOR US BECAUSE...

_____

_____

_____

_____

_____

_____

_____

MAKE IT F*CKING HAPPEN: HOW? WHEN?

_____

_____

_____

_____

_____

_____

REVIEW

DATE COMPLETED: / /

WHAT HAPPENED? (PEOPLE MET, HIGH POINTS, EXPECTATIONS VS REALITY)

_____

_____

_____

_____

_____

_____

_____

_____

_____

BUDGET

$

ANTICIPATED DATE

/ / TO / /

ACTION LIST

⊘ _____

⊘ _____

⊘ _____

⊘ _____

⊘ _____

⊘ _____

⊘ _____

⊘ _____

⊘ _____

⊘ _____

⊘ _____

Success! ✓

ONCE COMPLETE, PLACE A CHECK HERE
TO TAKE IT OFF YOUR BUCKET LIST

RATE THIS ACTIVITY

☆ ☆ ☆ ☆ ☆

ITEM #34:

SUMMARY: THIS WOULD BE F*CKING PERFECT FOR US BECAUSE...

_____

_____

_____

_____

_____

_____

MAKE IT F*CKING HAPPEN: HOW? WHEN?

_____

_____

_____

_____

_____

_____

_____

REVIEW

DATE COMPLETED: / /

WHAT HAPPENED? (PEOPLE MET, HIGH POINTS, EXPECTATIONS VS REALITY)

_____

_____

_____

_____

_____

_____

_____

_____

_____

BUDGET

$

ANTICIPATED DATE

/ /   TO   / /

ACTION LIST

- ⊘
- ⊘
- ⊘
- ⊘
- ⊘
- ⊘
- ⊘
- ⊘
- ⊘
- ⊘
- ⊘

Success! ✓

ONCE COMPLETE, PLACE A CHECK HERE
TO TAKE IT OFF YOUR BUCKET LIST

RATE THIS ACTIVITY

★ ★ ★ ★ ★

ITEM #35:

SUMMARY: THIS WOULD BE F*CKING PERFECT FOR US BECAUSE...

_____

_____

_____

_____

_____

_____

MAKE IT F*CKING HAPPEN: HOW? WHEN?

_____

_____

_____

_____

_____

_____

_____

REVIEW

DATE COMPLETED: / /

WHAT HAPPENED? (PEOPLE MET, HIGH POINTS, EXPECTATIONS VS REALITY)

_____

_____

_____

_____

_____

_____

_____

_____

_____

_____

BUDGET

$

ANTICIPATED DATE

/ /   TO   / /

ACTION LIST

- ⊘
- ⊘
- ⊘
- ⊘
- ⊘
- ⊘
- ⊘
- ⊘
- ⊘
- ⊘
- ⊘

Success!

✓

ONCE COMPLETE, PLACE A CHECK HERE
TO TAKE IT OFF YOUR BUCKET LIST

RATE THIS ACTIVITY

★★★★★

35

ITEM #36:

SUMMARY: THIS WOULD BE F*CKING PERFECT FOR US BECAUSE...

_____

_____

_____

_____

_____

_____

MAKE IT F*CKING HAPPEN: HOW? WHEN?

_____

_____

_____

_____

_____

_____

REVIEW

DATE COMPLETED: / /

WHAT HAPPENED? (PEOPLE MET, HIGH POINTS, EXPECTATIONS VS REALITY)

_____

_____

_____

_____

_____

_____

_____

_____

_____

BUDGET

$

ANTICIPATED DATE

/ /   TO   / /

ACTION LIST

- ⃝
- ⃝
- ⃝
- ⃝
- ⃝
- ⃝
- ⃝
- ⃝
- ⃝
- ⃝
- ⃝

Success! ✓

ONCE COMPLETE, PLACE A CHECK HERE
TO TAKE IT OFF YOUR BUCKET LIST

RATE THIS ACTIVITY

★★★★★

ITEM #37:

SUMMARY: THIS WOULD BE F*CKING PERFECT FOR US BECAUSE...

_____
_____
_____
_____
_____
_____

MAKE IT F*CKING HAPPEN: HOW? WHEN?

_____
_____
_____
_____
_____
_____
_____

BUDGET

$

ANTICIPATED DATE

/ / TO / /

ACTION LIST

- ⊘
- ⊘
- ⊘
- ⊘
- ⊘
- ⊘
- ⊘
- ⊘
- ⊘
- ⊘
- ⊘

REVIEW

DATE COMPLETED: / /

WHAT HAPPENED? (PEOPLE MET, HIGH POINTS, EXPECTATIONS VS REALITY)

_____
_____
_____
_____
_____
_____
_____
_____
_____

Success!

ONCE COMPLETE, PLACE A CHECK HERE
TO TAKE IT OFF YOUR BUCKET LIST

RATE THIS ACTIVITY

★ ★ ★ ★ ★

ITEM #38:

SUMMARY: THIS WOULD BE F*CKING PERFECT FOR US BECAUSE...

_____

_____

_____

_____

_____

_____

MAKE IT F*CKING HAPPEN: HOW? WHEN?

_____

_____

_____

_____

_____

_____

_____

BUDGET

$

ANTICIPATED DATE

/ /   TO   / /

ACTION LIST

- ⊘ _____
- ⊘ _____
- ⊘ _____
- ⊘ _____
- ⊘ _____
- ⊘ _____
- ⊘ _____
- ⊘ _____
- ⊘ _____
- ⊘ _____
- ⊘ _____

REVIEW

DATE COMPLETED: / /

WHAT HAPPENED? (PEOPLE MET, HIGH POINTS, EXPECTATIONS VS REALITY)

_____

_____

_____

_____

_____

_____

_____

_____

_____

Success! ✓

ONCE COMPLETE, PLACE A CHECK HERE
TO TAKE IT OFF YOUR BUCKET LIST

RATE THIS ACTIVITY

★ ★ ★ ★ ★

ITEM #39:

PRIORITY ★ ☆ ☆ ☆ ☆

SUMMARY: THIS WOULD BE F*CKING PERFECT FOR US BECAUSE...

_____
_____
_____
_____
_____
_____
_____

BUDGET

$

ANTICIPATED DATE

/ /   TO   / /

ACTION LIST

MAKE IT F*CKING HAPPEN: HOW? WHEN?

_____
_____
_____
_____
_____
_____
_____

REVIEW

DATE COMPLETED: / /

WHAT HAPPENED? (PEOPLE MET, HIGH POINTS, EXPECTATIONS VS REALITY)

_____
_____
_____
_____
_____
_____
_____
_____
_____

Success!

ONCE COMPLETE, PLACE A CHECK HERE
TO TAKE IT OFF YOUR BUCKET LIST

RATE THIS ACTIVITY

★ ★ ★ ★ ★

ITEM #40:

SUMMARY: THIS WOULD BE F*CKING PERFECT FOR US BECAUSE...

_____
_____
_____
_____
_____
_____

MAKE IT F*CKING HAPPEN: HOW? WHEN?

_____
_____
_____
_____
_____
_____

REVIEW

DATE COMPLETED: / /

WHAT HAPPENED? (PEOPLE MET, HIGH POINTS, EXPECTATIONS VS REALITY)

_____
_____
_____
_____
_____
_____
_____
_____

BUDGET

$

ANTICIPATED DATE

/ /   TO   / /

ACTION LIST

○ _____
○ _____
○ _____
○ _____
○ _____
○ _____
○ _____
○ _____
○ _____
○ _____
○ _____

Success! ✓

ONCE COMPLETE, PLACE A CHECK HERE
TO TAKE IT OFF YOUR BUCKET LIST

RATE THIS ACTIVITY

★★★★★

ITEM #41:

PRIORITY ★ ★ ★ ★ ★

SUMMARY: THIS WOULD BE F*CKING PERFECT FOR US BECAUSE...

BUDGET

$

ANTICIPATED DATE

/ /   TO   / /

ACTION LIST

MAKE IT F*CKING HAPPEN: HOW? WHEN?

REVIEW

DATE COMPLETED: / /

WHAT HAPPENED? (PEOPLE MET, HIGH POINTS, EXPECTATIONS VS REALITY)

Success!

ONCE COMPLETE, PLACE A CHECK HERE
TO TAKE IT OFF YOUR BUCKET LIST

RATE THIS ACTIVITY

★ ★ ★ ★ ★

ITEM #42:

PRIORITY ★★★★★

SUMMARY: THIS WOULD BE F*CKING PERFECT FOR US BECAUSE...

_____

_____

_____

_____

_____

_____

_____

MAKE IT F*CKING HAPPEN: HOW? WHEN?

_____

_____

_____

_____

_____

_____

REVIEW

DATE COMPLETED: /   /

WHAT HAPPENED? (PEOPLE MET, HIGH POINTS, EXPECTATIONS VS REALITY)

_____

_____

_____

_____

_____

_____

_____

_____

BUDGET

$

ANTICIPATED DATE

/   /   TO   /   /

ACTION LIST

⊘ _____
⊘ _____
⊘ _____
⊘ _____
⊘ _____
⊘ _____
⊘ _____
⊘ _____
⊘ _____
⊘ _____
⊘ _____

Success! ✓

ONCE COMPLETE, PLACE A CHECK HERE
TO TAKE IT OFF YOUR BUCKET LIST

RATE THIS ACTIVITY

★★★★★

ITEM #43:

PRIORITY ★ ★ ★ ★ ★

SUMMARY: THIS WOULD BE F*CKING PERFECT FOR US BECAUSE...

_____

_____

_____

_____

_____

_____

MAKE IT F*CKING HAPPEN: HOW? WHEN?

_____

_____

_____

_____

_____

BUDGET

$

ANTICIPATED DATE

/ / TO / /

ACTION LIST

- ⊘
- ⊘
- ⊘
- ⊘
- ⊘
- ⊘
- ⊘
- ⊘
- ⊘
- ⊘
- ⊘

REVIEW

DATE COMPLETED: / /

WHAT HAPPENED? (PEOPLE MET, HIGH POINTS, EXPECTATIONS VS REALITY)

_____

_____

_____

_____

_____

_____

_____

_____

_____

Success!

✓

ONCE COMPLETE, PLACE A CHECK HERE
TO TAKE IT OFF YOUR BUCKET LIST

RATE THIS ACTIVITY

★ ★ ★ ★ ★

ITEM #44:

SUMMARY: THIS WOULD BE F*CKING PERFECT FOR US BECAUSE...

_____

_____

_____

_____

_____

_____

_____

BUDGET

$

ANTICIPATED DATE

/ /   TO   / /

ACTION LIST

- ⊘ _____
- ⊘ _____
- ⊘ _____
- ⊘ _____
- ⊘ _____
- ⊘ _____
- ⊘ _____
- ⊘ _____
- ⊘ _____
- ⊘ _____
- ⊘ _____

MAKE IT F*CKING HAPPEN: HOW? WHEN?

_____

_____

_____

_____

_____

_____

_____

REVIEW

DATE COMPLETED: / /

WHAT HAPPENED? (PEOPLE MET, HIGH POINTS, EXPECTATIONS VS REALITY)

_____

_____

_____

_____

_____

_____

_____

_____

_____

_____

Success! ✓

ONCE COMPLETE, PLACE A CHECK HERE
TO TAKE IT OFF YOUR BUCKET LIST

RATE THIS ACTIVITY

★ ★ ★ ★ ★

ITEM #45:

SUMMARY: THIS WOULD BE F*CKING PERFECT FOR US BECAUSE...

_____

_____

_____

_____

_____

_____

MAKE IT F*CKING HAPPEN: HOW? WHEN?

_____

_____

_____

_____

_____

_____

BUDGET

$

ANTICIPATED DATE

/ / TO / /

ACTION LIST

- ⊘
- ⊘
- ⊘
- ⊘
- ⊘
- ⊘
- ⊘
- ⊘
- ⊘
- ⊘
- ⊘

REVIEW

DATE COMPLETED: / /

WHAT HAPPENED? (PEOPLE MET, HIGH POINTS, EXPECTATIONS VS REALITY)

_____

_____

_____

_____

_____

_____

_____

_____

_____

_____

Success! ✓

ONCE COMPLETE, PLACE A CHECK HERE
TO TAKE IT OFF YOUR BUCKET LIST

RATE THIS ACTIVITY

★ ★ ★ ★ ★

ITEM #46:

SUMMARY: THIS WOULD BE F*CKING PERFECT FOR US BECAUSE...

_____

_____

_____

_____

_____

_____

_____

MAKE IT F*CKING HAPPEN: HOW? WHEN?

_____

_____

_____

_____

_____

_____

_____

REVIEW

DATE COMPLETED: / /

WHAT HAPPENED? (PEOPLE MET, HIGH POINTS, EXPECTATIONS VS REALITY)

_____

_____

_____

_____

_____

_____

_____

_____

_____

_____

BUDGET

$

ANTICIPATED DATE

/ / TO / /

ACTION LIST

- ⊘
- ⊘
- ⊘
- ⊘
- ⊘
- ⊘
- ⊘
- ⊘
- ⊘
- ⊘
- ⊘

Success!

ONCE COMPLETE, PLACE A CHECK HERE
TO TAKE IT OFF YOUR BUCKET LIST

RATE THIS ACTIVITY

⭐ ⭐ ⭐ ⭐ ⭐

ITEM #47:

SUMMARY: THIS WOULD BE F*CKING PERFECT FOR US BECAUSE...

_____

_____

_____

_____

_____

_____

MAKE IT F*CKING HAPPEN: HOW? WHEN?

_____

_____

_____

_____

_____

REVIEW

DATE COMPLETED: / /

WHAT HAPPENED? (PEOPLE MET, HIGH POINTS, EXPECTATIONS VS REALITY)

_____

_____

_____

_____

_____

_____

_____

_____

_____

_____

BUDGET

$

ANTICIPATED DATE

/ /   TO   / /

ACTION LIST

- ⊘
- ⊘
- ⊘
- ⊘
- ⊘
- ⊘
- ⊘
- ⊘
- ⊘
- ⊘
- ⊘

Success!

✓

ONCE COMPLETE, PLACE A CHECK HERE
TO TAKE IT OFF YOUR BUCKET LIST

RATE THIS ACTIVITY

★ ★ ★ ★ ★

ITEM #48:

SUMMARY: THIS WOULD BE F*CKING PERFECT FOR US BECAUSE...

_____

_____

_____

_____

_____

_____

MAKE IT F*CKING HAPPEN: HOW? WHEN?

_____

_____

_____

_____

_____

_____

BUDGET

$

ANTICIPATED DATE

/ /   TO   / /

ACTION LIST

- ⊘
- ⊘
- ⊘
- ⊘
- ⊘
- ⊘
- ⊘
- ⊘
- ⊘
- ⊘
- ⊘

REVIEW

DATE COMPLETED: / /

WHAT HAPPENED? (PEOPLE MET, HIGH POINTS, EXPECTATIONS VS REALITY)

_____

_____

_____

_____

_____

_____

_____

_____

Success!

ONCE COMPLETE, PLACE A CHECK HERE
TO TAKE IT OFF YOUR BUCKET LIST

RATE THIS ACTIVITY

★ ★ ★ ★ ★

ITEM #49:

PRIORITY ★ ★ ★ ★ ★

SUMMARY: THIS WOULD BE F*CKING PERFECT FOR US BECAUSE...

_____
_____
_____
_____
_____
_____
_____

MAKE IT F*CKING HAPPEN: HOW? WHEN?

_____
_____
_____
_____
_____
_____
_____

REVIEW

DATE COMPLETED: / /

WHAT HAPPENED? (PEOPLE MET, HIGH POINTS, EXPECTATIONS VS REALITY)

_____
_____
_____
_____
_____
_____
_____
_____

BUDGET
$

ANTICIPATED DATE
/ /   TO   / /

ACTION LIST

- ⊘
- ⊘
- ⊘
- ⊘
- ⊘
- ⊘
- ⊘
- ⊘
- ⊘
- ⊘
- ⊘

Success! ✓

ONCE COMPLETE, PLACE A CHECK HERE
TO TAKE IT OFF YOUR BUCKET LIST

RATE THIS ACTIVITY

★ ★ ★ ★ ★

ITEM #50:

SUMMARY: THIS WOULD BE F*CKING PERFECT FOR US BECAUSE...

_____
_____
_____
_____
_____
_____
_____

MAKE IT F*CKING HAPPEN: HOW? WHEN?

_____
_____
_____
_____
_____
_____
_____

REVIEW

DATE COMPLETED: / /

WHAT HAPPENED? (PEOPLE MET, HIGH POINTS, EXPECTATIONS VS REALITY)

_____
_____
_____
_____
_____
_____
_____
_____
_____

BUDGET

$

ANTICIPATED DATE

/ / TO / /

ACTION LIST

- ⊘
- ⊘
- ⊘
- ⊘
- ⊘
- ⊘
- ⊘
- ⊘
- ⊘
- ⊘
- ⊘

Success! ✓

ONCE COMPLETE, PLACE A CHECK HERE
TO TAKE IT OFF YOUR BUCKET LIST

RATE THIS ACTIVITY

★ ★ ★ ★ ★

ITEM #51:

SUMMARY: THIS WOULD BE F*CKING PERFECT FOR US BECAUSE...

_____
_____
_____
_____
_____
_____

MAKE IT F*CKING HAPPEN: HOW? WHEN?

_____
_____
_____
_____
_____
_____

BUDGET

$

ANTICIPATED DATE

/ /   TO   / /

ACTION LIST

- ⊘ _____
- ⊘ _____
- ⊘ _____
- ⊘ _____
- ⊘ _____
- ⊘ _____
- ⊘ _____
- ⊘ _____
- ⊘ _____
- ⊘ _____
- ⊘ _____

REVIEW

DATE COMPLETED: / /

WHAT HAPPENED? (PEOPLE MET, HIGH POINTS, EXPECTATIONS VS REALITY)

_____
_____
_____
_____
_____
_____
_____
_____

Success! ✓

ONCE COMPLETE, PLACE A CHECK HERE
TO TAKE IT OFF YOUR BUCKET LIST

RATE THIS ACTIVITY

★★★★★

ITEM #52:

SUMMARY: THIS WOULD BE F*CKING PERFECT FOR US BECAUSE...

_____
_____
_____
_____
_____
_____
_____

MAKE IT F*CKING HAPPEN: HOW? WHEN?

_____
_____
_____
_____
_____
_____
_____

BUDGET

$

ANTICIPATED DATE

/ /   TO   / /

ACTION LIST

- ⊘
- ⊘
- ⊘
- ⊘
- ⊘
- ⊘
- ⊘
- ⊘
- ⊘
- ⊘
- ⊘

REVIEW

DATE COMPLETED: / /

WHAT HAPPENED? (PEOPLE MET, HIGH POINTS, EXPECTATIONS VS REALITY)

_____
_____
_____
_____
_____
_____
_____
_____
_____

Success! ✓

ONCE COMPLETE, PLACE A CHECK HERE
TO TAKE IT OFF YOUR BUCKET LIST

RATE THIS ACTIVITY

★★★★★

ITEM #53:

PRIORITY ★ ★ ★ ★ ★

SUMMARY: THIS WOULD BE F*CKING PERFECT FOR US BECAUSE...

_____
_____
_____
_____
_____
_____
_____

BUDGET
$

ANTICIPATED DATE

/ /   TO   / /

ACTION LIST

⊘ _____
⊘ _____
⊘ _____
⊘ _____
⊘ _____
⊘ _____
⊘ _____
⊘ _____
⊘ _____
⊘ _____
⊘ _____

MAKE IT F*CKING HAPPEN: HOW? WHEN?

_____
_____
_____
_____
_____
_____
_____

REVIEW

DATE COMPLETED: / /

WHAT HAPPENED? (PEOPLE MET, HIGH POINTS, EXPECTATIONS VS REALITY)

_____
_____
_____
_____
_____
_____
_____
_____
_____
_____

Success!

✓

ONCE COMPLETE, PLACE A CHECK HERE
TO TAKE IT OFF YOUR BUCKET LIST

RATE THIS ACTIVITY

★ ★ ★ ★ ★

ITEM #54:

SUMMARY: THIS WOULD BE F*CKING PERFECT FOR US BECAUSE...

_____

_____

_____

_____

_____

_____

MAKE IT F*CKING HAPPEN: HOW? WHEN?

_____

_____

_____

_____

_____

_____

REVIEW

DATE COMPLETED: / /

WHAT HAPPENED? (PEOPLE MET, HIGH POINTS, EXPECTATIONS VS REALITY)

_____

_____

_____

_____

_____

_____

_____

_____

BUDGET

$

ANTICIPATED DATE

/ / TO / /

ACTION LIST

- ⊘
- ⊘
- ⊘
- ⊘
- ⊘
- ⊘
- ⊘
- ⊘
- ⊘
- ⊘
- ⊘

Success!

ONCE COMPLETE, PLACE A CHECK HERE
TO TAKE IT OFF YOUR BUCKET LIST

RATE THIS ACTIVITY

★ ★ ★ ★ ★

54

ITEM #55:

SUMMARY: THIS WOULD BE F*CKING PERFECT FOR US BECAUSE...

_____

_____

_____

_____

_____

_____

MAKE IT F*CKING HAPPEN: HOW? WHEN?

_____

_____

_____

_____

_____

_____

REVIEW

DATE COMPLETED: / /

WHAT HAPPENED? (PEOPLE MET, HIGH POINTS, EXPECTATIONS VS REALITY)

_____

_____

_____

_____

_____

_____

_____

_____

_____

BUDGET

$

ANTICIPATED DATE

/ /   TO   / /

ACTION LIST

- ⊘
- ⊘
- ⊘
- ⊘
- ⊘
- ⊘
- ⊘
- ⊘
- ⊘
- ⊘
- ⊘

Success!

✓

ONCE COMPLETE, PLACE A CHECK HERE
TO TAKE IT OFF YOUR BUCKET LIST

RATE THIS ACTIVITY

★ ★ ★ ★ ★

ITEM #56:

BUDGET

$

ANTICIPATED DATE

/ /   TO   / /

SUMMARY: THIS WOULD BE F*CKING PERFECT FOR US BECAUSE...

_____

_____

_____

_____

_____

_____

ACTION LIST

MAKE IT F*CKING HAPPEN: HOW? WHEN?

_____

_____

_____

_____

_____

_____

REVIEW

DATE COMPLETED: / /

WHAT HAPPENED? (PEOPLE MET, HIGH POINTS, EXPECTATIONS VS REALITY)

_____

_____

_____

_____

_____

_____

_____

_____

_____

_____

Success!

ONCE COMPLETE, PLACE A CHECK HERE
TO TAKE IT OFF YOUR BUCKET LIST

RATE THIS ACTIVITY

★ ★ ★ ★ ★

ITEM #57:

SUMMARY: THIS WOULD BE F*CKING PERFECT FOR US BECAUSE...

_____

_____

_____

_____

_____

_____

MAKE IT F*CKING HAPPEN: HOW? WHEN?

_____

_____

_____

_____

_____

_____

_____

REVIEW

DATE COMPLETED: / /

WHAT HAPPENED? (PEOPLE MET, HIGH POINTS, EXPECTATIONS VS REALITY)

_____

_____

_____

_____

_____

_____

_____

_____

_____

_____

BUDGET

$

ANTICIPATED DATE

/ /   TO   / /

ACTION LIST

⊘
⊘
⊘
⊘
⊘
⊘
⊘
⊘
⊘
⊘
⊘

Success!

✓

ONCE COMPLETE, PLACE A CHECK HERE
TO TAKE IT OFF YOUR BUCKET LIST

RATE THIS ACTIVITY

★ ★ ★ ★ ★

ITEM #58:

SUMMARY: THIS WOULD BE F*CKING PERFECT FOR US BECAUSE...

_____
_____
_____
_____
_____
_____
_____

MAKE IT F*CKING HAPPEN: HOW? WHEN?

_____
_____
_____
_____
_____
_____
_____

BUDGET
$

ANTICIPATED DATE
/ /   TO   / /

ACTION LIST

- ⊘
- ⊘
- ⊘
- ⊘
- ⊘
- ⊘
- ⊘
- ⊘
- ⊘
- ⊘
- ⊘

REVIEW

DATE COMPLETED: / /

WHAT HAPPENED? (PEOPLE MET, HIGH POINTS, EXPECTATIONS VS REALITY)

_____
_____
_____
_____
_____
_____
_____
_____
_____

Success! ✓

ONCE COMPLETE, PLACE A CHECK HERE
TO TAKE IT OFF YOUR BUCKET LIST

RATE THIS ACTIVITY

★ ★ ★ ★ ★

ITEM #59:

PRIORITY ★ ★ ★ ★ ★

SUMMARY: THIS WOULD BE F*CKING PERFECT FOR US BECAUSE...

_____

_____

_____

_____

_____

_____

_____

BUDGET

$

ANTICIPATED DATE

/ /   TO   / /

ACTION LIST

⊘ _____

⊘ _____

⊘ _____

⊘ _____

⊘ _____

⊘ _____

⊘ _____

⊘ _____

⊘ _____

⊘ _____

⊘ _____

MAKE IT F*CKING HAPPEN: HOW? WHEN?

_____

_____

_____

_____

_____

_____

_____

REVIEW

DATE COMPLETED: / /

WHAT HAPPENED? (PEOPLE MET, HIGH POINTS, EXPECTATIONS VS REALITY)

_____

_____

_____

_____

_____

_____

_____

_____

_____

_____

Success!

ONCE COMPLETE, PLACE A CHECK HERE
TO TAKE IT OFF YOUR BUCKET LIST

RATE THIS ACTIVITY

★ ★ ★ ★ ★

ITEM #60:

SUMMARY: THIS WOULD BE F*CKING PERFECT FOR US BECAUSE...

BUDGET

$

ANTICIPATED DATE

/ /   TO   / /

MAKE IT F*CKING HAPPEN: HOW? WHEN?

ACTION LIST

⊘
⊘
⊘
⊘
⊘
⊘
⊘
⊘
⊘
⊘
⊘

REVIEW

DATE COMPLETED: / /

WHAT HAPPENED? (PEOPLE MET, HIGH POINTS, EXPECTATIONS VS REALITY)

Success!

ONCE COMPLETE, PLACE A CHECK HERE
TO TAKE IT OFF YOUR BUCKET LIST

RATE THIS ACTIVITY

★ ★ ★ ★ ★

ITEM #61:

SUMMARY: THIS WOULD BE F*CKING PERFECT FOR US BECAUSE...

_____
_____
_____
_____
_____
_____

MAKE IT F*CKING HAPPEN: HOW? WHEN?

_____
_____
_____
_____
_____
_____

REVIEW
DATE COMPLETED: /   /

WHAT HAPPENED? (PEOPLE MET, HIGH POINTS, EXPECTATIONS VS REALITY)

_____
_____
_____
_____
_____
_____
_____
_____
_____

BUDGET
$

ANTICIPATED DATE

/ /   TO   / /

ACTION LIST

- ⊘
- ⊘
- ⊘
- ⊘
- ⊘
- ⊘
- ⊘
- ⊘
- ⊘
- ⊘
- ⊘

Success!

✓

ONCE COMPLETE, PLACE A CHECK HERE
TO TAKE IT OFF YOUR BUCKET LIST

RATE THIS ACTIVITY

★ ★ ★ ★ ★

ITEM #62:

SUMMARY: THIS WOULD BE F*CKING PERFECT FOR US BECAUSE...

_____

_____

_____

_____

_____

_____

MAKE IT F*CKING HAPPEN: HOW? WHEN?

_____

_____

_____

_____

_____

_____

_____

REVIEW

DATE COMPLETED: / /

WHAT HAPPENED? (PEOPLE MET, HIGH POINTS, EXPECTATIONS VS REALITY)

_____

_____

_____

_____

_____

_____

_____

_____

BUDGET

$

ANTICIPATED DATE

/ / TO / /

ACTION LIST

⊘
⊘
⊘
⊘
⊘
⊘
⊘
⊘
⊘
⊘
⊘

Success!

ONCE COMPLETE, PLACE A CHECK HERE
TO TAKE IT OFF YOUR BUCKET LIST

RATE THIS ACTIVITY

★★★★★

ITEM #63:

SUMMARY: THIS WOULD BE F*CKING PERFECT FOR US BECAUSE...

_____

_____

_____

_____

_____

_____

BUDGET

$

ANTICIPATED DATE

/ /   TO   / /

ACTION LIST

- ⊘
- ⊘
- ⊘
- ⊘
- ⊘
- ⊘
- ⊘
- ⊘
- ⊘
- ⊘
- ⊘

MAKE IT F*CKING HAPPEN: HOW? WHEN?

_____

_____

_____

_____

_____

_____

REVIEW   DATE COMPLETED: / /

WHAT HAPPENED? (PEOPLE MET, HIGH POINTS, EXPECTATIONS VS REALITY)

_____

_____

_____

_____

_____

_____

_____

_____

Success! ✓

ONCE COMPLETE, PLACE A CHECK HERE
TO TAKE IT OFF YOUR BUCKET LIST

RATE THIS ACTIVITY

★ ★ ★ ★ ★

ITEM #64:

PRIORITY ★ ★ ★ ★ ★

SUMMARY: THIS WOULD BE F*CKING PERFECT FOR US BECAUSE...

_____

_____

_____

_____

_____

_____

_____

MAKE IT F*CKING HAPPEN: HOW? WHEN?

_____

_____

_____

_____

_____

_____

_____

REVIEW

DATE COMPLETED: / /

WHAT HAPPENED? (PEOPLE MET, HIGH POINTS, EXPECTATIONS VS REALITY)

_____

_____

_____

_____

_____

_____

_____

_____

BUDGET

$

ANTICIPATED DATE

/ /   TO   / /

ACTION LIST

- ⃠
- ⃠
- ⃠
- ⃠
- ⃠
- ⃠
- ⃠
- ⃠
- ⃠
- ⃠
- ⃠

Success! ✓

ONCE COMPLETE, PLACE A CHECK HERE
TO TAKE IT OFF YOUR BUCKET LIST

RATE THIS ACTIVITY

★ ★ ★ ★ ★

ITEM #65:

PRIORITY ★ ★ ★ ★ ★

SUMMARY: THIS WOULD BE F*CKING PERFECT FOR US BECAUSE...

_____
_____
_____
_____
_____
_____

BUDGET

$

ANTICIPATED DATE

/ / TO / /

ACTION LIST

○ _____
○ _____
○ _____
○ _____
○ _____
○ _____
○ _____
○ _____
○ _____
○ _____
○ _____

MAKE IT F*CKING HAPPEN: HOW? WHEN?

_____
_____
_____
_____
_____
_____
_____

REVIEW

DATE COMPLETED: / /

WHAT HAPPENED? (PEOPLE MET, HIGH POINTS, EXPECTATIONS VS REALITY)

_____
_____
_____
_____
_____
_____
_____
_____
_____
_____

Success!

✓

ONCE COMPLETE, PLACE A CHECK HERE
TO TAKE IT OFF YOUR BUCKET LIST

RATE THIS ACTIVITY

★ ★ ★ ★ ★

65

ITEM #66:

PRIORITY ★ ★ ★ ★ ★

SUMMARY: THIS WOULD BE F*CKING PERFECT FOR US BECAUSE...

_____
_____
_____
_____
_____
_____
_____

MAKE IT F*CKING HAPPEN: HOW? WHEN?

_____
_____
_____
_____
_____
_____

BUDGET

$

ANTICIPATED DATE

/ /   TO   / /

ACTION LIST

- ⊘
- ⊘
- ⊘
- ⊘
- ⊘
- ⊘
- ⊘
- ⊘
- ⊘
- ⊘
- ⊘

REVIEW

DATE COMPLETED: / /

WHAT HAPPENED? (PEOPLE MET, HIGH POINTS, EXPECTATIONS VS REALITY)

_____
_____
_____
_____
_____
_____
_____
_____
_____

Success!

✓

ONCE COMPLETE, PLACE A CHECK HERE
TO TAKE IT OFF YOUR BUCKET LIST

RATE THIS ACTIVITY

★ ★ ★ ★ ★

ITEM #67:

PRIORITY ★ ★ ★ ★ ★

SUMMARY: THIS WOULD BE F*CKING PERFECT FOR US BECAUSE...

_____

_____

_____

_____

_____

_____

BUDGET

$

ANTICIPATED DATE

/ /   TO   / /

MAKE IT F*CKING HAPPEN: HOW? WHEN?

_____

_____

_____

_____

_____

_____

_____

ACTION LIST

- ⊘
- ⊘
- ⊘
- ⊘
- ⊘
- ⊘
- ⊘
- ⊘
- ⊘
- ⊘
- ⊘

REVIEW

DATE COMPLETED: / /

WHAT HAPPENED? (PEOPLE MET, HIGH POINTS, EXPECTATIONS VS REALITY)

_____

_____

_____

_____

_____

_____

_____

_____

_____

_____

Success!

✓

ONCE COMPLETE, PLACE A CHECK HERE
TO TAKE IT OFF YOUR BUCKET LIST

RATE THIS ACTIVITY

★ ★ ★ ★ ★

ITEM #68:

PRIORITY ★ ★ ★ ★ ★

SUMMARY: THIS WOULD BE F*CKING PERFECT FOR US BECAUSE...

_____

_____

_____

_____

_____

_____

_____

BUDGET

$

ANTICIPATED DATE

/ /   TO   / /

ACTION LIST

- ⊘
- ⊘
- ⊘
- ⊘
- ⊘
- ⊘
- ⊘
- ⊘
- ⊘
- ⊘
- ⊘

MAKE IT F*CKING HAPPEN: HOW? WHEN?

_____

_____

_____

_____

_____

_____

_____

REVIEW

DATE COMPLETED: / /

WHAT HAPPENED? (PEOPLE MET, HIGH POINTS, EXPECTATIONS VS REALITY)

_____

_____

_____

_____

_____

_____

_____

_____

_____

Success!

ONCE COMPLETE, PLACE A CHECK HERE
TO TAKE IT OFF YOUR BUCKET LIST

RATE THIS ACTIVITY

★ ★ ★ ★ ★

ITEM #69:

BUDGET

$

ANTICIPATED DATE

/ /   TO   / /

SUMMARY: THIS WOULD BE F*CKING PERFECT FOR US BECAUSE...

_____

_____

_____

_____

_____

ACTION LIST

- ⊘
- ⊘
- ⊘
- ⊘
- ⊘
- ⊘
- ⊘
- ⊘
- ⊘
- ⊘
- ⊘

MAKE IT F*CKING HAPPEN: HOW? WHEN?

_____

_____

_____

_____

_____

_____

REVIEW   DATE COMPLETED: / /

WHAT HAPPENED? (PEOPLE MET, HIGH POINTS, EXPECTATIONS VS REALITY)

_____

_____

_____

_____

_____

_____

_____

_____

Success! ✓

ONCE COMPLETE, PLACE A CHECK HERE
TO TAKE IT OFF YOUR BUCKET LIST

RATE THIS ACTIVITY

★ ★ ★ ★ ★

ITEM #70:

SUMMARY: THIS WOULD BE F*CKING PERFECT FOR US BECAUSE...

_____

_____

_____

_____

_____

_____

_____

MAKE IT F*CKING HAPPEN: HOW? WHEN?

_____

_____

_____

_____

_____

_____

REVIEW

DATE COMPLETED: / /

WHAT HAPPENED? (PEOPLE MET, HIGH POINTS, EXPECTATIONS VS REALITY)

_____

_____

_____

_____

_____

_____

_____

_____

BUDGET

$

ANTICIPATED DATE

/ / TO / /

ACTION LIST

- ⊘
- ⊘
- ⊘
- ⊘
- ⊘
- ⊘
- ⊘
- ⊘
- ⊘
- ⊘
- ⊘

Success!

ONCE COMPLETE, PLACE A CHECK HERE
TO TAKE IT OFF YOUR BUCKET LIST

RATE THIS ACTIVITY

★★★★★

70

ITEM #71:

SUMMARY: THIS WOULD BE F*CKING PERFECT FOR US BECAUSE...

_____

_____

_____

_____

_____

_____

BUDGET

$

ANTICIPATED DATE

/ /   TO   / /

ACTION LIST

MAKE IT F*CKING HAPPEN: HOW? WHEN?

_____

_____

_____

_____

_____

_____

_____

REVIEW

DATE COMPLETED: / /

WHAT HAPPENED? (PEOPLE MET, HIGH POINTS, EXPECTATIONS VS REALITY)

_____

_____

_____

_____

_____

_____

_____

_____

Success!

ONCE COMPLETE, PLACE A CHECK HERE
TO TAKE IT OFF YOUR BUCKET LIST

RATE THIS ACTIVITY

★ ★ ★ ★ ★

ITEM #72:

SUMMARY: THIS WOULD BE F*CKING PERFECT FOR US BECAUSE...

_____

_____

_____

_____

_____

_____

BUDGET

$

ANTICIPATED DATE

/ /   TO   / /

ACTION LIST

⊘ _____
⊘ _____
⊘ _____
⊘ _____
⊘ _____
⊘ _____
⊘ _____
⊘ _____
⊘ _____
⊘ _____
⊘ _____

MAKE IT F*CKING HAPPEN: HOW? WHEN?

_____

_____

_____

_____

_____

_____

_____

REVIEW

DATE COMPLETED: / /

WHAT HAPPENED? (PEOPLE MET, HIGH POINTS, EXPECTATIONS VS REALITY)

_____

_____

_____

_____

_____

_____

_____

_____

_____

Success! ✓

ONCE COMPLETE, PLACE A CHECK HERE
TO TAKE IT OFF YOUR BUCKET LIST

RATE THIS ACTIVITY

★ ★ ★ ★ ★

ITEM #73:

SUMMARY: THIS WOULD BE F*CKING PERFECT FOR US BECAUSE...

_____

_____

_____

_____

_____

_____

MAKE IT F*CKING HAPPEN: HOW? WHEN?

_____

_____

_____

_____

_____

_____

REVIEW

DATE COMPLETED: / /

WHAT HAPPENED? (PEOPLE MET, HIGH POINTS, EXPECTATIONS VS REALITY)

_____

_____

_____

_____

_____

_____

_____

_____

BUDGET

$

ANTICIPATED DATE

/ /　TO　/ /

ACTION LIST

⊘
⊘
⊘
⊘
⊘
⊘
⊘
⊘
⊘
⊘
⊘

Success! ✓

ONCE COMPLETE, PLACE A CHECK HERE
TO TAKE IT OFF YOUR BUCKET LIST

RATE THIS ACTIVITY

★ ★ ★ ★ ★

ITEM #74:

SUMMARY: THIS WOULD BE F*CKING PERFECT FOR US BECAUSE...

_____
_____
_____
_____
_____
_____
_____

MAKE IT F*CKING HAPPEN: HOW? WHEN?

_____
_____
_____
_____
_____
_____
_____
_____

REVIEW

DATE COMPLETED: / /

WHAT HAPPENED? (PEOPLE MET, HIGH POINTS, EXPECTATIONS VS REALITY)

_____
_____
_____
_____
_____
_____
_____
_____
_____

BUDGET

$

ANTICIPATED DATE

/ / TO / /

ACTION LIST

- ⊘
- ⊘
- ⊘
- ⊘
- ⊘
- ⊘
- ⊘
- ⊘
- ⊘
- ⊘
- ⊘

Success! ✓

ONCE COMPLETE, PLACE A CHECK HERE
TO TAKE IT OFF YOUR BUCKET LIST

RATE THIS ACTIVITY

★ ★ ★ ★ ★

ITEM #75:

SUMMARY: THIS WOULD BE F*CKING PERFECT FOR US BECAUSE...

_____
_____
_____
_____
_____
_____
_____

MAKE IT F*CKING HAPPEN: HOW? WHEN?

_____
_____
_____
_____
_____
_____
_____

BUDGET

$

ANTICIPATED DATE

/ /   TO   / /

ACTION LIST

- ⊘
- ⊘
- ⊘
- ⊘
- ⊘
- ⊘
- ⊘
- ⊘
- ⊘
- ⊘
- ⊘

REVIEW

DATE COMPLETED: / /

WHAT HAPPENED? (PEOPLE MET, HIGH POINTS, EXPECTATIONS VS REALITY)

_____
_____
_____
_____
_____
_____
_____
_____
_____
_____

Success!

✓

ONCE COMPLETE, PLACE A CHECK HERE
TO TAKE IT OFF YOUR BUCKET LIST

RATE THIS ACTIVITY

★ ★ ★ ★ ★

ITEM #76:

PRIORITY ☆☆☆☆☆

SUMMARY: THIS WOULD BE F*CKING PERFECT FOR US BECAUSE...

_____

_____

_____

_____

_____

_____

_____

MAKE IT F*CKING HAPPEN: HOW? WHEN?

_____

_____

_____

_____

_____

_____

_____

BUDGET

$

ANTICIPATED DATE

/ / TO / /

ACTION LIST

⊘ _____

⊘ _____

⊘ _____

⊘ _____

⊘ _____

⊘ _____

⊘ _____

⊘ _____

⊘ _____

⊘ _____

⊘ _____

REVIEW

DATE COMPLETED: / /

WHAT HAPPENED? (PEOPLE MET, HIGH POINTS, EXPECTATIONS VS REALITY)

_____

_____

_____

_____

_____

_____

_____

_____

_____

_____

_____

Success! ✓

ONCE COMPLETE, PLACE A CHECK HERE
TO TAKE IT OFF YOUR BUCKET LIST

RATE THIS ACTIVITY

★★★★★

ITEM #77:

SUMMARY: THIS WOULD BE F*CKING PERFECT FOR US BECAUSE...

_____

_____

_____

_____

_____

_____

BUDGET

$

ANTICIPATED DATE

/ /   TO   / /

ACTION LIST

MAKE IT F*CKING HAPPEN: HOW? WHEN?

_____

_____

_____

_____

_____

_____

_____

REVIEW

DATE COMPLETED: / /

WHAT HAPPENED? (PEOPLE MET, HIGH POINTS, EXPECTATIONS VS REALITY)

_____

_____

_____

_____

_____

_____

_____

_____

_____

_____

Success!

ONCE COMPLETE, PLACE A CHECK HERE
TO TAKE IT OFF YOUR BUCKET LIST

RATE THIS ACTIVITY

★ ★ ★ ★ ★

ITEM #78:

SUMMARY: THIS WOULD BE F*CKING PERFECT FOR US BECAUSE...

_____

_____

_____

_____

_____

_____

_____

MAKE IT F*CKING HAPPEN: HOW? WHEN?

_____

_____

_____

_____

_____

_____

_____

BUDGET

$

ANTICIPATED DATE

/ / TO / /

ACTION LIST

- ⊘ _____
- ⊘ _____
- ⊘ _____
- ⊘ _____
- ⊘ _____
- ⊘ _____
- ⊘ _____
- ⊘ _____
- ⊘ _____
- ⊘ _____
- ⊘ _____

REVIEW

DATE COMPLETED: / /

WHAT HAPPENED? (PEOPLE MET, HIGH POINTS, EXPECTATIONS VS REALITY)

_____

_____

_____

_____

_____

_____

_____

_____

_____

_____

Success! ✓

ONCE COMPLETE, PLACE A CHECK HERE
TO TAKE IT OFF YOUR BUCKET LIST

RATE THIS ACTIVITY

★ ★ ★ ★ ★

ITEM #79:

SUMMARY: THIS WOULD BE F*CKING PERFECT FOR US BECAUSE...

_____
_____
_____
_____
_____
_____

BUDGET

$

ANTICIPATED DATE

/ /   TO   / /

ACTION LIST

- ⊘ _____
- ⊘ _____
- ⊘ _____
- ⊘ _____
- ⊘ _____
- ⊘ _____
- ⊘ _____
- ⊘ _____
- ⊘ _____
- ⊘ _____

MAKE IT F*CKING HAPPEN: HOW? WHEN?

_____
_____
_____
_____
_____
_____

REVIEW

DATE COMPLETED: / /

WHAT HAPPENED? (PEOPLE MET, HIGH POINTS, EXPECTATIONS VS REALITY)

_____
_____
_____
_____
_____
_____
_____
_____
_____
_____

Success!
✓

ONCE COMPLETE, PLACE A CHECK HERE
TO TAKE IT OFF YOUR BUCKET LIST

RATE THIS ACTIVITY

★ ★ ★ ★ ★

ITEM #80:

PRIORITY ★★★★★

SUMMARY: THIS WOULD BE F*CKING PERFECT FOR US BECAUSE...

_____
_____
_____
_____
_____
_____
_____

BUDGET

$

ANTICIPATED DATE

/ /   TO   / /

ACTION LIST

⊘ _____
⊘ _____
⊘ _____
⊘ _____
⊘ _____
⊘ _____
⊘ _____
⊘ _____
⊘ _____
⊘ _____
⊘ _____

MAKE IT F*CKING HAPPEN: HOW? WHEN?

_____
_____
_____
_____
_____
_____
_____
_____

REVIEW

DATE COMPLETED: / /

WHAT HAPPENED? (PEOPLE MET, HIGH POINTS, EXPECTATIONS VS REALITY)

_____
_____
_____
_____
_____
_____
_____
_____
_____
_____

Success! ✓

ONCE COMPLETE, PLACE A CHECK HERE
TO TAKE IT OFF YOUR BUCKET LIST

RATE THIS ACTIVITY

★★★★★

ITEM #81:

SUMMARY: THIS WOULD BE F*CKING PERFECT FOR US BECAUSE...

_____

_____

_____

_____

_____

_____

MAKE IT F*CKING HAPPEN: HOW? WHEN?

_____

_____

_____

_____

_____

_____

REVIEW   DATE COMPLETED: / /

WHAT HAPPENED? (PEOPLE MET, HIGH POINTS, EXPECTATIONS VS REALITY)

_____

_____

_____

_____

_____

_____

_____

_____

_____

BUDGET

$

ANTICIPATED DATE

/ /   TO   / /

ACTION LIST

- ⊘
- ⊘
- ⊘
- ⊘
- ⊘
- ⊘
- ⊘
- ⊘
- ⊘
- ⊘
- ⊘

Success!

✓

ONCE COMPLETE, PLACE A CHECK HERE
TO TAKE IT OFF YOUR BUCKET LIST

RATE THIS ACTIVITY

★ ★ ★ ★ ★

ITEM #82:

PRIORITY ★★★★★

SUMMARY: THIS WOULD BE F*CKING PERFECT FOR US BECAUSE...

_____
_____
_____
_____
_____
_____
_____

MAKE IT F*CKING HAPPEN: HOW? WHEN?

_____
_____
_____
_____
_____
_____

BUDGET
$

ANTICIPATED DATE
/ / TO / /

ACTION LIST

- ⊘
- ⊘
- ⊘
- ⊘
- ⊘
- ⊘
- ⊘
- ⊘
- ⊘
- ⊘
- ⊘

REVIEW

DATE COMPLETED: / /

WHAT HAPPENED? (PEOPLE MET, HIGH POINTS, EXPECTATIONS VS REALITY)

_____
_____
_____
_____
_____
_____
_____
_____
_____

Success! ✓

ONCE COMPLETE, PLACE A CHECK HERE
TO TAKE IT OFF YOUR BUCKET LIST

RATE THIS ACTIVITY

★★★★★

ITEM #83:

SUMMARY: THIS WOULD BE F*CKING PERFECT FOR US BECAUSE...

_____
_____
_____
_____
_____
_____
_____

MAKE IT F*CKING HAPPEN: HOW? WHEN?

_____
_____
_____
_____
_____
_____
_____
_____

REVIEW

DATE COMPLETED: /   /

WHAT HAPPENED? (PEOPLE MET, HIGH POINTS, EXPECTATIONS VS REALITY)

_____
_____
_____
_____
_____
_____
_____
_____
_____
_____
_____

BUDGET

$

ANTICIPATED DATE

/ /   TO   / /

ACTION LIST

- ⊘
- ⊘
- ⊘
- ⊘
- ⊘
- ⊘
- ⊘
- ⊘
- ⊘
- ⊘
- ⊘

Success! ✓

ONCE COMPLETE, PLACE A CHECK HERE
TO TAKE IT OFF YOUR BUCKET LIST

RATE THIS ACTIVITY

★ ★ ★ ★ ★

ITEM #84:

SUMMARY: THIS WOULD BE F*CKING PERFECT FOR US BECAUSE...

_____
_____
_____
_____
_____
_____
_____

MAKE IT F*CKING HAPPEN: HOW? WHEN?

_____
_____
_____
_____
_____
_____

BUDGET

$

ANTICIPATED DATE

/ / TO / /

ACTION LIST

- ⊘
- ⊘
- ⊘
- ⊘
- ⊘
- ⊘
- ⊘
- ⊘
- ⊘
- ⊘
- ⊘

REVIEW

DATE COMPLETED: / /

WHAT HAPPENED? (PEOPLE MET, HIGH POINTS, EXPECTATIONS VS REALITY)

_____
_____
_____
_____
_____
_____
_____
_____
_____

Success! ✓

ONCE COMPLETE, PLACE A CHECK HERE
TO TAKE IT OFF YOUR BUCKET LIST

RATE THIS ACTIVITY

★ ★ ★ ★ ★

ITEM #85:

SUMMARY: THIS WOULD BE F*CKING PERFECT FOR US BECAUSE...

_____
_____
_____
_____
_____
_____
_____

MAKE IT F*CKING HAPPEN: HOW? WHEN?

_____
_____
_____
_____
_____
_____
_____

BUDGET
$

ANTICIPATED DATE
/ /   TO   / /

ACTION LIST

◯
◯
◯
◯
◯
◯
◯
◯
◯
◯
◯

REVIEW

DATE COMPLETED: / /

WHAT HAPPENED? (PEOPLE MET, HIGH POINTS, EXPECTATIONS VS REALITY)

_____
_____
_____
_____
_____
_____
_____
_____
_____
_____

Success!
✓

ONCE COMPLETE, PLACE A CHECK HERE
TO TAKE IT OFF YOUR BUCKET LIST

RATE THIS ACTIVITY

★ ★ ★ ★ ★

ITEM #86:

PRIORITY ★★★★★

SUMMARY: THIS WOULD BE F*CKING PERFECT FOR US BECAUSE...

_____
_____
_____
_____
_____
_____
_____

MAKE IT F*CKING HAPPEN: HOW? WHEN?

_____
_____
_____
_____
_____
_____

REVIEW

DATE COMPLETED: / /

WHAT HAPPENED? (PEOPLE MET, HIGH POINTS, EXPECTATIONS VS REALITY)

_____
_____
_____
_____
_____
_____
_____
_____
_____

BUDGET

$

ANTICIPATED DATE

/ /   TO   / /

ACTION LIST

- ⊘
- ⊘
- ⊘
- ⊘
- ⊘
- ⊘
- ⊘
- ⊘
- ⊘
- ⊘
- ⊘

Success!

✓

ONCE COMPLETE, PLACE A CHECK HERE
TO TAKE IT OFF YOUR BUCKET LIST

RATE THIS ACTIVITY

★★★★★

ITEM #87:

SUMMARY: THIS WOULD BE F*CKING PERFECT FOR US BECAUSE...

_____
_____
_____
_____
_____
_____
_____

BUDGET
$

ANTICIPATED DATE
/ /   TO   / /

ACTION LIST

⊘ _____
⊘ _____
⊘ _____
⊘ _____
⊘ _____
⊘ _____
⊘ _____
⊘ _____
⊘ _____
⊘ _____
⊘ _____

MAKE IT F*CKING HAPPEN: HOW? WHEN?

_____
_____
_____
_____
_____
_____

REVIEW

DATE COMPLETED: / /

WHAT HAPPENED? (PEOPLE MET, HIGH POINTS, EXPECTATIONS VS REALITY)

_____
_____
_____
_____
_____
_____
_____
_____
_____

Success!

ONCE COMPLETE, PLACE A CHECK HERE
TO TAKE IT OFF YOUR BUCKET LIST

RATE THIS ACTIVITY

★★★★★

ITEM #88:

SUMMARY: THIS WOULD BE F*CKING PERFECT FOR US BECAUSE...

_____

_____

_____

_____

_____

_____

_____

MAKE IT F*CKING HAPPEN: HOW? WHEN?

_____

_____

_____

_____

_____

_____

REVIEW

DATE COMPLETED: / /

WHAT HAPPENED? (PEOPLE MET, HIGH POINTS, EXPECTATIONS VS REALITY)

_____

_____

_____

_____

_____

_____

_____

_____

BUDGET

$

ANTICIPATED DATE

/ / TO / /

ACTION LIST

- ⊘
- ⊘
- ⊘
- ⊘
- ⊘
- ⊘
- ⊘
- ⊘
- ⊘
- ⊘
- ⊘

Success!

✓

ONCE COMPLETE, PLACE A CHECK HERE
TO TAKE IT OFF YOUR BUCKET LIST

RATE THIS ACTIVITY

★ ★ ★ ★ ★

ITEM #89:

SUMMARY: THIS WOULD BE F*CKING PERFECT FOR US BECAUSE...

_____
_____
_____
_____
_____
_____

BUDGET

$

ANTICIPATED DATE

/ /   TO   / /

ACTION LIST

- ⊘ _____
- ⊘ _____
- ⊘ _____
- ⊘ _____
- ⊘ _____
- ⊘ _____
- ⊘ _____
- ⊘ _____
- ⊘ _____
- ⊘ _____
- ⊘ _____

MAKE IT F*CKING HAPPEN: HOW? WHEN?

_____
_____
_____
_____
_____
_____
_____

REVIEW

DATE COMPLETED: / /

WHAT HAPPENED? (PEOPLE MET, HIGH POINTS, EXPECTATIONS VS REALITY)

_____
_____
_____
_____
_____
_____
_____
_____
_____

Success!

✓

ONCE COMPLETE, PLACE A CHECK HERE
TO TAKE IT OFF YOUR BUCKET LIST

RATE THIS ACTIVITY

★ ★ ★ ★ ★

ITEM #90:

SUMMARY: THIS WOULD BE F*CKING PERFECT FOR US BECAUSE...

_____

_____

_____

_____

_____

_____

_____

MAKE IT F*CKING HAPPEN: HOW? WHEN?

_____

_____

_____

_____

_____

_____

_____

REVIEW

DATE COMPLETED: / /

WHAT HAPPENED? (PEOPLE MET, HIGH POINTS, EXPECTATIONS VS REALITY)

_____

_____

_____

_____

_____

_____

_____

_____

BUDGET

$

ANTICIPATED DATE

/ /   TO   / /

ACTION LIST

- ⊘
- ⊘
- ⊘
- ⊘
- ⊘
- ⊘
- ⊘
- ⊘
- ⊘
- ⊘
- ⊘

Success!

ONCE COMPLETE, PLACE A CHECK HERE
TO TAKE IT OFF YOUR BUCKET LIST

RATE THIS ACTIVITY

★★★★★

ITEM #91:

SUMMARY: THIS WOULD BE F*CKING PERFECT FOR US BECAUSE...

_____
_____
_____
_____
_____
_____
_____

BUDGET

$

ANTICIPATED DATE

/ /   TO   / /

ACTION LIST

MAKE IT F*CKING HAPPEN: HOW? WHEN?

_____
_____
_____
_____
_____
_____
_____

REVIEW

DATE COMPLETED: / /

WHAT HAPPENED? (PEOPLE MET, HIGH POINTS, EXPECTATIONS VS REALITY)

_____
_____
_____
_____
_____
_____
_____
_____
_____
_____
_____

Success!

ONCE COMPLETE, PLACE A CHECK HERE
TO TAKE IT OFF YOUR BUCKET LIST

RATE THIS ACTIVITY

★ ★ ★ ★ ★

ITEM #92:

SUMMARY: THIS WOULD BE F*CKING PERFECT FOR US BECAUSE...

_____

_____

_____

_____

_____

_____

_____

MAKE IT F*CKING HAPPEN: HOW? WHEN?

_____

_____

_____

_____

_____

_____

REVIEW

DATE COMPLETED: / /

WHAT HAPPENED? (PEOPLE MET, HIGH POINTS, EXPECTATIONS VS REALITY)

_____

_____

_____

_____

_____

_____

_____

_____

_____

BUDGET

$

ANTICIPATED DATE

/ / TO / /

ACTION LIST

- ⊘
- ⊘
- ⊘
- ⊘
- ⊘
- ⊘
- ⊘
- ⊘
- ⊘
- ⊘
- ⊘

Success! ✓

ONCE COMPLETE, PLACE A CHECK HERE
TO TAKE IT OFF YOUR BUCKET LIST

RATE THIS ACTIVITY

★★★★★

ITEM #93:

SUMMARY: THIS WOULD BE F*CKING PERFECT FOR US BECAUSE...

_____
_____
_____
_____
_____
_____

MAKE IT F*CKING HAPPEN: HOW? WHEN?

_____
_____
_____
_____
_____
_____

REVIEW

DATE COMPLETED: / /

WHAT HAPPENED? (PEOPLE MET, HIGH POINTS, EXPECTATIONS VS REALITY)

_____
_____
_____
_____
_____
_____
_____
_____

BUDGET

$

ANTICIPATED DATE

/ /   TO   / /

ACTION LIST

⊘
⊘
⊘
⊘
⊘
⊘
⊘
⊘
⊘
⊘
⊘

Success!

✓

ONCE COMPLETE, PLACE A CHECK HERE
TO TAKE IT OFF YOUR BUCKET LIST

RATE THIS ACTIVITY

★ ★ ★ ★ ★

ITEM #94:

SUMMARY: THIS WOULD BE F*CKING PERFECT FOR US BECAUSE...

_____
_____
_____
_____
_____
_____
_____

MAKE IT F*CKING HAPPEN: HOW? WHEN?

_____
_____
_____
_____
_____
_____

BUDGET

$

ANTICIPATED DATE

/ /   TO   / /

ACTION LIST

- ⊘
- ⊘
- ⊘
- ⊘
- ⊘
- ⊘
- ⊘
- ⊘
- ⊘
- ⊘
- ⊘

REVIEW

DATE COMPLETED: / /

WHAT HAPPENED? (PEOPLE MET, HIGH POINTS, EXPECTATIONS VS REALITY)

_____
_____
_____
_____
_____
_____
_____
_____
_____

Success!

✓

ONCE COMPLETE, PLACE A CHECK HERE
TO TAKE IT OFF YOUR BUCKET LIST

RATE THIS ACTIVITY

★ ★ ★ ★ ★

ITEM #95:

SUMMARY: THIS WOULD BE F*CKING PERFECT FOR US BECAUSE...

_____

_____

_____

_____

_____

_____

_____

MAKE IT F*CKING HAPPEN: HOW? WHEN?

_____

_____

_____

_____

_____

_____

_____

_____

REVIEW

DATE COMPLETED: /   /

WHAT HAPPENED? (PEOPLE MET, HIGH POINTS, EXPECTATIONS VS REALITY)

_____

_____

_____

_____

_____

_____

_____

_____

_____

_____

BUDGET

$

ANTICIPATED DATE

/   /   TO   /   /

ACTION LIST

- ⊘
- ⊘
- ⊘
- ⊘
- ⊘
- ⊘
- ⊘
- ⊘
- ⊘
- ⊘
- ⊘

Success!

✓

ONCE COMPLETE, PLACE A CHECK HERE
TO TAKE IT OFF YOUR BUCKET LIST

RATE THIS ACTIVITY

★★★★★

ITEM #96:

PRIORITY ★★★★★

SUMMARY: THIS WOULD BE F*CKING PERFECT FOR US BECAUSE...

_____
_____
_____
_____
_____
_____
_____
_____

MAKE IT F*CKING HAPPEN: HOW? WHEN?

_____
_____
_____
_____
_____
_____
_____

BUDGET

$

ANTICIPATED DATE

/ /   TO   / /

ACTION LIST

- ⊘
- ⊘
- ⊘
- ⊘
- ⊘
- ⊘
- ⊘
- ⊘
- ⊘
- ⊘
- ⊘

REVIEW

DATE COMPLETED: / /

WHAT HAPPENED? (PEOPLE MET, HIGH POINTS, EXPECTATIONS VS REALITY)

_____
_____
_____
_____
_____
_____
_____
_____
_____

Success! ✓

ONCE COMPLETE, PLACE A CHECK HERE
TO TAKE IT OFF YOUR BUCKET LIST

RATE THIS ACTIVITY

★★★★★

ITEM #97:

SUMMARY: THIS WOULD BE F*CKING PERFECT FOR US BECAUSE...

_____
_____
_____
_____
_____
_____

MAKE IT F*CKING HAPPEN: HOW? WHEN?

_____
_____
_____
_____
_____
_____

REVIEW

DATE COMPLETED: / /

WHAT HAPPENED? (PEOPLE MET, HIGH POINTS, EXPECTATIONS VS REALITY)

_____
_____
_____
_____
_____
_____
_____
_____
_____
_____

BUDGET
$

ANTICIPATED DATE
/ / TO / /

ACTION LIST

- ⊘
- ⊘
- ⊘
- ⊘
- ⊘
- ⊘
- ⊘
- ⊘
- ⊘
- ⊘
- ⊘

Success! ✓

ONCE COMPLETE, PLACE A CHECK HERE
TO TAKE IT OFF YOUR BUCKET LIST

RATE THIS ACTIVITY

★ ★ ★ ★ ★

ITEM #98:

PRIORITY ★★★★★

SUMMARY: THIS WOULD BE F*CKING PERFECT FOR US BECAUSE...

_____
_____
_____
_____
_____
_____
_____

MAKE IT F*CKING HAPPEN: HOW? WHEN?

_____
_____
_____
_____
_____
_____
_____

REVIEW

DATE COMPLETED: / /

WHAT HAPPENED? (PEOPLE MET, HIGH POINTS, EXPECTATIONS VS REALITY)

_____
_____
_____
_____
_____
_____
_____
_____
_____
_____

BUDGET

$

ANTICIPATED DATE

/ /   TO   / /

ACTION LIST

⊘
⊘
⊘
⊘
⊘
⊘
⊘
⊘
⊘
⊘
⊘

Success!

✓

ONCE COMPLETE, PLACE A CHECK HERE
TO TAKE IT OFF YOUR BUCKET LIST

RATE THIS ACTIVITY

★★★★★

ITEM #99:

PRIORITY ★ ★ ★ ★ ★

SUMMARY: THIS WOULD BE F*CKING PERFECT FOR US BECAUSE...

_____

_____

_____

_____

_____

_____

BUDGET

$

ANTICIPATED DATE

/ /   TO   / /

ACTION LIST

- ⊘ _____
- ⊘ _____
- ⊘ _____
- ⊘ _____
- ⊘ _____
- ⊘ _____
- ⊘ _____
- ⊘ _____
- ⊘ _____
- ⊘ _____
- ⊘ _____

MAKE IT F*CKING HAPPEN: HOW? WHEN?

_____

_____

_____

_____

_____

_____

REVIEW

DATE COMPLETED: / /

WHAT HAPPENED? (PEOPLE MET, HIGH POINTS, EXPECTATIONS VS REALITY)

_____

_____

_____

_____

_____

_____

_____

_____

_____

_____

_____

Success!

✓

ONCE COMPLETE, PLACE A CHECK HERE
TO TAKE IT OFF YOUR BUCKET LIST

RATE THIS ACTIVITY

★ ★ ★ ★ ★

ITEM #100:

SUMMARY: THIS WOULD BE F*CKING PERFECT FOR US BECAUSE...

_____

_____

_____

_____

_____

_____

_____

MAKE IT F*CKING HAPPEN: HOW? WHEN?

_____

_____

_____

_____

_____

_____

_____

_____

REVIEW

DATE COMPLETED: /   /

WHAT HAPPENED? (PEOPLE MET, HIGH POINTS, EXPECTATIONS VS REALITY)

_____

_____

_____

_____

_____

_____

_____

_____

_____

BUDGET

$

ANTICIPATED DATE

/ /   TO   / /

ACTION LIST

- ⊘
- ⊘
- ⊘
- ⊘
- ⊘
- ⊘
- ⊘
- ⊘
- ⊘
- ⊘
- ⊘

Success! ✓

ONCE COMPLETE, PLACE A CHECK HERE
TO TAKE IT OFF YOUR BUCKET LIST

RATE THIS ACTIVITY

★ ★ ★ ★ ★

(100)

ITEM #101:

SUMMARY: THIS WOULD BE F*CKING PERFECT FOR US BECAUSE...

_____

_____

_____

_____

_____

_____

_____

MAKE IT F*CKING HAPPEN: HOW? WHEN?

_____

_____

_____

_____

_____

_____

_____

BUDGET
$
ANTICIPATED DATE
/ /   TO   / /

ACTION LIST

- ⊘
- ⊘
- ⊘
- ⊘
- ⊘
- ⊘
- ⊘
- ⊘
- ⊘
- ⊘
- ⊘

REVIEW

DATE COMPLETED: / /

WHAT HAPPENED? (PEOPLE MET, HIGH POINTS, EXPECTATIONS VS REALITY)

_____

_____

_____

_____

_____

_____

_____

_____

_____

_____

Success!

✓

ONCE COMPLETE, PLACE A CHECK HERE
TO TAKE IT OFF YOUR BUCKET LIST

RATE THIS ACTIVITY

★★★★★

THE PERFECT COMPANION
THE F*CK IT! MONTHLY CALENDAR PLANNER

✔ **Goal Planning**: Establish a series of long-term goals for the year, with prompts to summarize goal outcomes, reasons and required resources. Include a drawing, picture or text to visualize your goal.

✔ **Goal Progress Chart**: At at-a-glance view of each major goal's progress. Monitor your journey to goal accomplishment with this simple bar chart.

✔ **Exploring Goal Setting**: These pages are an opportunity to pause and reflect on opportunities for self-improvement through goal achievement. Explore ways that others have inspired you; identify personal characteristics and qualities that will help you accomplish goals; and develop a tangible vision of what goal accomplishment will look like for you.

✔ **Goal Check-In**: At the end of each month, you'll be guided to reflect on your goals' progress on the Goal Check-In page. This page includes three important questions to help stay accountable to your plan, and reinforces the importance of the goals you've set. These questions are designed to prompt internal dialog and self-reflection about your goal's progress, and reinvigorate commitment over the coming month.

✔ **Monitor progress using your Monthly Goal Progress chart**: Shade in the completion scale for particular goals to give yourself a visual reinforcement of progress and success.

✔ **Goal Setting Word Prompts**: A fun activity to help inspire new goals or flesh out ideas for self-improvement. This list contains 600+ seed words to prompt development of goal statements and/or contemplate themes not previously considered.

✔ **Monthly Dream Board**: Compiling your monthly vision board helps visualize what can be accomplished in the short term. Collage together photos, clippings, drawings, and quotes to envision goals and inspire commitment.

IN STOCK NOW AT AMAZON.COM

bit.ly/goalweekly

Made in the USA
Coppell, TX
27 April 2020